Using Interactive Digital Games for Early Learning in Preschool

Copyright © My First Picture Book Inc. by Prof. Ava Thompson

All rights reserved.

No portion of this book may be reproduced in any form without written permission from the publisher or author, except as permitted by Canadian and U.S. copyright law.

This publication is designed to provide accurate and authoritative information in regard to the subject matter covered. It is sold with the understanding that neither the author nor the publisher is engaged in rendering legal, investment, accounting or other professional services. While the publisher and author have used their best efforts in preparing this book, they make no representations or warranties with respect to the accuracy or completeness of the contents of this book and specifically disclaim any implied warranties of merchantability or fitness for a particular purpose. No warranty may be created or extended by sales representatives or written sales materials. The advice and strategies contained herein may not be suitable for your situation. You should consult with a professional when appropriate. Neither the publisher nor the author shall be liable for any loss of profit or any other commercial damages, including but not limited to special, incidental, consequential, personal, or other damages.

Contents

Introduction to Interactive Digital Games in Preschool — 1
1. Importance of incorporating technology in early learning — 3
2. Benefits of using interactive digital games in preschool education — 5
3. Research supporting the use of digital games for early learning — 8
4. How digital games align with the developmental needs of preschoolers — 11

Understanding Preschool Learning Objectives — 13
5. Key learning objectives in preschool education — 15
6. Importance of play-based learning in early childhood — 17
7. How digital games can support the achievement of learning objectives — 19
8. Aligning digital games with specific learning goals — 21
9. Strategies for integrating digital games into the curriculum — 23

Selecting and Evaluating Interactive Digital Games — 25
10. Criteria for selecting high-quality interactive digital games — 27
11. Evaluating the educational value of digital games — 30
12. Considering age-appropriateness and skill levels in game selection — 32
13. Exploring different types of digital games for preschoolers — 35
14. Resources for finding and reviewing interactive digital games — 38

Designing Effective Learning Experiences with Digital Games — 40
15. Principles of effective game-based learning design — 42
16. Integrating digital games into lesson plans and activities — 44
17. Creating interactive and engaging learning experiences with games — 46

18.	Incorporating assessment and feedback mechanisms in game design	48
19.	Adapting games to meet individual student needs	50

Supporting Social and Emotional Development through Digital Games — 52

20.	Understanding the importance of social and emotional skills in preschool	54
21.	How digital games can enhance social and emotional development	56
22.	Addressing empathy, cooperation, and conflict resolution through games	58
23.	Promoting self-regulation and emotional expression with digital games	61
24.	Strategies for fostering social interactions during game-based learning	63

Enhancing Cognitive Skills with Interactive Digital Games — 66

25.	Cognitive skills development in early childhood	68
26.	Cognitive benefits of using digital games in preschool education	70
27.	Enhancing memory, attention, and problem-solving through games	73
28.	Promoting critical thinking and creativity with digital games	75
29.	Strategies for incorporating cognitive skill development in game-based learning	77

Promoting Language and Literacy with Digital Games — 80

30.	Importance of language and literacy development in preschool	82
31.	How digital games can facilitate language acquisition and literacy skills	84
32.	Supporting vocabulary development through game-based learning	86
33.	Promoting phonological awareness and early reading skills with games	88
34.	Integrating digital storytelling and writing activities in game-based learning	90

Encouraging Physical Activity and Motor Skills through Digital Games — 93

35.	Importance of physical activity and motor skills development in preschool	95
36.	How digital games can promote physical movement and coordination	97

37.	Integrating active play and exercise in game-based learning	99
38.	Using motion-controlled games to enhance motor skill development	101
39.	Strategies for balancing screen time with physical activity in preschool	103

Engaging Parents and Caregivers in Game-Based Learning		106
40.	Importance of involving parents and caregivers in preschool education	108
41.	Strategies for communicating the benefits of game-based learning to parents	110
42.	Involving parents in game selection and monitoring screen time	113
43.	Encouraging parent-child interactions through digital games	115
44.	Resources and support for parents to extend learning beyond the classroom	117

Overcoming Challenges and Addressing Concerns		119
45.	Common challenges and concerns related to using digital games in preschool	121
46.	Strategies for managing screen time and ensuring appropriate use of technology	123
47.	Addressing potential barriers to implementing game-based learning	126
48.	Supporting professional development for teachers in using digital games	129
49.	Digital Safety, Ethics, and Cultural Sensitivity in Game-Based Learning	131
50.	Global Perspectives on Digital Game-Based Learning	134
51.	Technology Integration Roadmap for Schools and Educators	137

Future Trends and Considerations in Interactive Digital Games for Early Learning		140
52.	Emerging trends in educational technology and digital games	142
53.	Innovations in interactive game design for early learning	145
54.	Anticipating changes in preschool education landscapes	148
55.	Preparing for future advancements and challenges in digital game-based learning	151

Introduction to Interactive Digital Games in Preschool

In this era of rapid technological advancement, the incorporation of interactive digital games into preschool education marks a significant stride in aligning early learning with the demands of the digital age. This introduction serves as a gateway to understanding the multifaceted impact of technology in early childhood education, focusing on the benefits and effectiveness of interactive digital games in preschool settings.

The essence of integrating technology in early learning lies in providing young learners with the tools and skills necessary for thriving in a digitally-driven world. Early exposure to technology, when thoughtfully implemented, can significantly enhance learning experiences, spur creativity, and cultivate essential skills such as critical thinking and problem-solving. This introduction delves into the reasons behind this integration, emphasizing the need for a balance between digital and traditional learning methods. It also explores how appropriately used technology can facilitate cognitive development and prepare children for future technological landscapes.

Further, the use of interactive digital games in preschool education offers a range of educational benefits. These games transform complex concepts into accessible and enjoyable activities, creating a dynamic learning environment where children can explore, experiment, and learn at their own pace. Among the key benefits are heightened engagement, improved hand-eye coordination, enhanced problem-solving skills, and the development of basic computer literacy. Supported by case studies and examples, this introduction will highlight the successful application of game-based learning in preschools.

Additionally, a growing body of research supports the positive impact of digital games on early learning. Well-designed educational games have been shown to improve memory, attention, language skills, and even contribute to social and emotional development. This introduction will review current research findings, providing evidence of the effectiveness of digital games in early childhood education and discussing their alignment with educational standards and learning objectives.

Lastly, it's crucial to recognize that preschoolers learn best through play and exploration. Digital games, when carefully selected, can align with the developmental needs of these young learners, offering an interactive and sensory-rich environment conducive to learning at this age. The introduction will cover how digital games can be tailored to suit different developmental stages, focusing on aspects like motor skill development, cognitive growth, language acquisition, and social-emotional learning, while also addressing the importance of choosing age-appropriate games that match the learning pace and interests of young children.

In summary, this introduction sets the stage for a comprehensive exploration of interactive digital games in preschool education, highlighting their crucial role in modern early learning environments. By understanding and applying these concepts, educators and parents can significantly enhance the educational experiences of preschoolers, preparing them effectively for a future that is increasingly intertwined with technology.

1

IMPORTANCE OF INCORPORATING TECHNOLOGY IN EARLY LEARNING

In the rapidly evolving digital age, the integration of technology into early childhood education is not just a trend but a critical component of modern teaching methods. This imperative change offers young learners an invaluable head start in developing the skills required in a world increasingly dominated by digital interactions and processes. When introduced thoughtfully and appropriately, technology can significantly enhance the learning experiences of preschool children, fostering an environment that nurtures creativity, and develops foundational skills in critical thinking and problem-solving.

Embracing Technology in Early Learning

The early years of a child's life are pivotal for cognitive, social, and emotional development. In these formative years, children are exceptionally receptive to learning new skills. Introducing technology during this stage provides a unique opportunity to harness their innate curiosity and adaptability. By integrating digital tools and resources in educational settings, we can create interactive, engaging, and stimulating learning experiences that resonate with young learners.

However, it's crucial to approach this integration with a balance. While technology can be a powerful learning aid, it should not replace traditional, hands-on, and play-based learning methods that are essential for early development. Instead, the goal should be to create a blended learning environment where digital and traditional methods coexist harmoniously and complement each other.

Enhancing Learning Experiences

The thoughtful incorporation of technology in early education can transform traditional learning paradigms. Interactive digital games, educational apps, and e-books can turn abstract concepts into tangible experiences, making learning more engaging and less intimidating for young minds. These digital tools also offer personalized learning experiences, allowing children to learn at their own pace, thus catering to individual learning styles and needs.

In the realm of creativity, technology serves as a canvas for imagination. Digital art tools, storytelling apps, and music composition software can unlock new avenues for creative expression, encouraging children to explore and develop their artistic abilities.

Developing Foundational Skills

One of the most significant benefits of integrating technology in early learning is the development of critical foundational skills. Digital games and activities designed for preschoolers often involve problem-solving tasks, logical reasoning challenges, and puzzles that enhance cognitive abilities. These activities stimulate the brain and foster analytical thinking, an essential skill in all areas of learning and everyday life.

Moreover, technology introduces young children to the basics of digital literacy. Navigating through interactive games and apps, children develop an understanding of how to interact with digital interfaces, a skill that is becoming as fundamental as reading and writing in today's world.

Preparing for the Future

The early introduction of technology also plays a vital role in preparing children for future educational endeavors and the digital workplace. As technology continues to advance, the ability to adapt and be comfortable with new digital tools and platforms will be crucial for success in almost every field. By integrating technology into early childhood education, we are not only enhancing current learning experiences but also laying a foundation for lifelong adaptability and success in a rapidly changing digital landscape.

In conclusion, incorporating technology into early learning is a step towards equipping young learners with the skills, creativity, and adaptability needed to thrive in the 21st century. By striking the right balance between digital and traditional learning methods, and focusing on the developmental appropriateness of technology, we can create enriching, engaging, and effective learning experiences for preschoolers. This section sets the stage for the book, outlining why and how technology can be a powerful ally in early childhood education.

2

BENEFITS OF USING INTERACTIVE DIGITAL GAMES IN PRESCHOOL EDUCATION

Interactive digital games have become a significant component in the realm of preschool education, offering an array of benefits that extend far beyond mere entertainment. These games transform learning into an engaging, enjoyable, and interactive experience, making complex concepts more accessible and fun for young learners. In a preschool setting, where exploration and experimentation are key, digital games provide a unique environment that aligns perfectly with the learning style and pace of young children.

Enhanced Engagement and Motivation

One of the most striking benefits of integrating interactive digital games in preschool education is the noticeable increase in student engagement and motivation. Traditional educational methods, while effective, might not always capture the diverse interests of young children. Digital games, with their vibrant animations, engaging narratives, and interactive challenges, captivate children's attention, drawing them into a world of learning that feels more like play than work.

For example, games like "Endless Alphabet" use colorful monsters to teach letter recognition and vocabulary. Children are motivated to drag letters into place, with each letter making its own unique sound, turning the process of learning to read into a fun and interactive experience.

Improved Hand-Eye Coordination

Digital games are excellent tools for developing hand-eye coordination in preschoolers. Games that require children to interact with a device, like tapping, swiping, or dragging objects on a screen, help refine their motor skills. These skills are crucial for later academic tasks, such as writing and drawing.

A popular game in this category is "Fruit Ninja," where children use their fingers to slice fruit that appears on the screen. This simple action helps them develop coordination and precision, skills that are foundational for more complex tasks.

Development of Problem-Solving Skills

Interactive digital games are particularly effective in enhancing problem-solving skills. Many games present challenges that require thinking, strategizing, and making decisions to achieve objectives. This type of gameplay is instrumental in fostering critical thinking and analytical skills.

For instance, games like "Lego Duplo World" offer a series of challenges that encourage children to think creatively. They need to build structures, solve puzzles, and navigate through stories, which helps develop their problem-solving abilities and creativity.

Fostering Basic Computer Literacy

In an increasingly digital world, early exposure to technology through games helps preschoolers develop basic computer literacy. Navigating through game interfaces, understanding how to use touchscreens or mouse-and-keyboard setups, and recognizing common digital symbols are all skills that prepare children for the technology-driven future.

Games like "Toca Boca" series are excellent for introducing young learners to digital interfaces. These games have intuitive interfaces designed for little fingers, allowing children to explore, experiment, and learn how to interact with digital devices.

Reinforcing Academic Skills

Interactive digital games can also be powerful tools for reinforcing academic skills such as mathematics, language, and science. They offer a playful approach to learning that can complement traditional classroom teaching.

For example, "ABCmouse.com" offers a comprehensive curriculum that covers a wide range of subjects. Through interactive games, the platform teaches reading, math, science, and art, making these subjects accessible and enjoyable for young minds.

Encouraging Social Interaction

While digital games are often criticized for being isolating, many are designed to encourage social interaction and teamwork. Games that allow for multiple players or that can be played in a classroom setting can foster collaboration and communication among preschoolers.

"Animal Jam," for instance, is a game that allows children to explore a virtual world where they can interact, play games, and learn about animals together. This kind of interactive play not only entertains but also teaches valuable social skills.

In conclusion, the use of interactive digital games in preschool education offers a multitude of benefits. From enhancing engagement and motivation to developing essential academic and life skills, these games are invaluable tools in the hands of educators. By selecting appropriate games and integrating them effectively into the curriculum, preschools can create a dynamic and enriching learning environment that prepares children for the challenges of the digital age.

3

RESEARCH SUPPORTING THE USE OF DIGITAL GAMES FOR EARLY LEARNING

The integration of digital games in early childhood education is supported by a substantial and growing body of research. These studies reveal that thoughtfully designed educational games can have a significant positive impact on various aspects of early learning. This includes improvements in cognitive abilities such as memory and attention, enhancements in language skills, and contributions to social and emotional development.

Cognitive Enhancements Through Digital Games

A significant area of research in the field of digital game-based learning is the development of cognitive skills. Several studies have shown that interactive digital games can notably improve memory and attention in young children. For instance, research published in early childhood education journals has demonstrated that games requiring pattern recognition and memory exercises can enhance short-term and working memory in preschoolers.

Games like "Peek-a-Zoo" by Duck Duck Moose are excellent examples of this. They engage children in activities that require identifying different animals and remembering their characteristics, thereby boosting memory and attention.

Language and Literacy Advancements

Digital games also play a pivotal role in language acquisition and literacy skills. The Joan Ganz Cooney Center's research highlights that digital games incorporating phonetics, vocabulary, and storytelling can significantly enrich a child's language skills. Interactive elements like voice narration and word recognition contribute to this development.

For example, the game "ABCya!" offers a range of literacy games that focus on letter recognition, phonetic sounds, and vocabulary building, aligning with the foundational language skills essential in early childhood education.

Promoting Social and Emotional Development

Another area where digital games have shown considerable benefits is in fostering social and emotional growth. Research indicates that games designed with cooperative play and problem-solving can help children develop empathy, understand emotions, and learn social interaction skills. These games often simulate real-life scenarios where children must work together or make decisions impacting others, thereby encouraging empathy and social understanding.

"Daniel Tiger's Grr-ific Feelings" is one such game that helps children understand and express their emotions. Through interactive storytelling and role-playing, children learn about empathy, sharing, and cooperation.

Aligning with Educational Standards

Digital games in early learning environments also stand out for their ability to align with educational standards and objectives. Educational researchers have pointed out that many digital games are explicitly designed to complement traditional curriculums, reinforcing the concepts and skills taught in the classroom. This alignment ensures that children are not only engaged in playing but are also learning and reinforcing essential academic skills.

The game "Starfall" is a prime example, offering activities that align with early education curriculums. It covers foundational skills in reading and mathematics, presented through interactive and entertaining game formats.

Global Research Perspectives

The effectiveness of digital games in early education is not limited to specific regions or countries. Global research has shown similar positive trends, indicating that regardless of the geographical and cultural context, digital games can be effective educational tools. Studies from various parts of the world support the notion that when integrated thoughtfully, digital games can be a universal tool for enhancing early childhood education.

In conclusion, the research supporting the use of digital games in early learning environments is compelling. It underscores that when chosen and implemented thoughtfully, these games can be powerful tools for enhancing various aspects of a child's development. By providing evidence of their effectiveness in improving cognitive skills, language and literacy development, and social and emotional growth, this research forms a strong foundation for the argument in favor of incorporating digital games into early childhood education programs.

4

How Digital Games Align with the Developmental Needs of Preschoolers

Preschoolers, in their prime years of exploration and learning, absorb information best through play. Digital games, when thoughtfully chosen, can align seamlessly with the developmental needs of children in this age group. They can offer an environment that is both interactive and sensory-rich, enhancing the learning experience in ways that are most effective for young children.

Aligning with Motor Skill Development

Fine motor skills are a crucial developmental aspect for preschoolers. Digital games can play a significant role in honing these skills. For instance, games that require children to use touchscreens involve actions like tapping, swiping, or dragging objects, all of which help develop hand-eye coordination and fine motor precision.

A game like "Toca Kitchen," where children pretend to cook and prepare meals, is an excellent example. It requires them to use their fingers to slice, mix, and cook virtual ingredients, thus refining their motor skills in a context that is both fun and engaging.

Supporting Cognitive Growth

Cognitive development in preschoolers involves developing skills such as problem-solving, memory, and logical thinking. Digital games that include puzzles, memory games, and problem-solving tasks are particularly beneficial for this aspect of development.

Games like "Lego Builder's Journey" offer puzzles that require children to think logically to build pathways or solve challenges, thereby enhancing their cognitive abilities. These games also help in developing spatial awareness and planning skills.

Enhancing Language Acquisition

Language acquisition is another critical area of development for preschoolers. Digital games that include storytelling, word recognition, and interactive conversations can significantly aid in language development.

An example is "Endless Alphabet," which introduces children to new words and their meanings through interactive puzzles. Each word is taught in context, with playful animations that make learning engaging and memorable.

Promoting Social-Emotional Learning

Social-emotional learning in early childhood lays the groundwork for how children understand and interact with others. Digital games that focus on cooperative play, understanding emotions, and social interactions can greatly support this area of development.

For example, "Daniel Tiger's Day & Night" helps children understand daily routines, feelings, and appropriate social behavior. The game uses familiar characters and scenarios to teach empathy, sharing, and cooperation.

Importance of Age-Appropriate Games

The effectiveness of digital games in meeting developmental needs largely depends on their appropriateness for the child's age. Games for preschoolers should be designed with their developmental stage in mind. This includes consideration of the game's complexity, the skills required to play, and the interests that are typical for the age group.

For instance, a game designed for a three-year-old would differ significantly from one intended for a five-year-old. The former might focus more on basic shape recognition and simple problem-solving, while the latter might incorporate more complex puzzles and basic math skills.

In summary, when digital games are carefully selected to align with the developmental stages of preschoolers, they can be highly effective tools for supporting growth in areas like motor skills, cognitive development, language acquisition, and social-emotional learning. It is essential, however, to choose games that are age-appropriate, matching the learning pace and interests of young children. By doing so, educators and parents can ensure that digital games serve as valuable and effective tools in the developmental journey of preschoolers.

Understanding Preschool Learning Objectives

In the fascinating and ever-evolving world of early childhood education, understanding and aligning with preschool learning objectives is a critical aspect of fostering holistic development in young learners. This introduction sets the stage for an in-depth exploration of the key learning objectives in preschool education, highlighting the crucial role of play-based learning and the innovative ways digital games can support and enhance these objectives.

Preschool education transcends beyond mere academic preparation; it's fundamentally about nurturing the all-around development of children. The learning objectives at this stage are multifaceted, encompassing social and emotional growth, language and communication skills, basic literacy and numeracy, as well as creativity and expression. Not to forget, physical development is also a cornerstone, focusing on both gross and fine motor skills which are essential for everyday activities.

Play-based learning, a pivotal concept in early childhood education, is effectively the foundation upon which children build their understanding of the world. It's through playful exploration that they develop key social dynamics, refine their language skills, and engage in critical problem-solving. Research consistently reinforces that children who partake in quality play-based learning are better equipped for future academic and social endeavors. For instance, role-playing games not only entertain but also instill empathy and social skills.

In this digital age, interactive digital games emerge as a potent tool in achieving these preschool learning objectives. These games, when thoughtfully designed and used, can target specific developmental skills like numeracy and literacy, while also fostering social-emotional abilities. Their interactive nature not only makes learning more engaging but can also provide a personalized experience through adaptive learning technologies.

However, the effective integration of digital games into preschool education requires careful alignment with specific learning goals. This means choosing games that are meticulously designed to develop certain skill sets or knowledge areas. For instance, a game focusing on phonetics can significantly bolster literacy objectives. It is imperative for educators to critically assess these games to ensure they align with educational standards and effectively meet the intended learning outcomes.

Strategically integrating digital games into the preschool curriculum demands more than just allowing children to play. It involves embedding these games within a structured learning framework, balancing them with traditional teaching methods, and setting clear objectives for their use. Continuous monitoring and adjustment of game use are crucial for assessing their effectiveness and suitability. Additionally, incorporating collaborative play and encouraging parental involvement can further enhance the learning experience.

As we delve into this topic, it becomes clear that understanding and strategically integrating digital games in line with preschool learning objectives can significantly enrich early education. By thoughtfully aligning these games with key developmental areas and embedding them into the curriculum, educators can craft a dynamic, engaging, and effective learning environment for preschoolers, setting a strong foundation for their future learning journey.

5

KEY LEARNING OBJECTIVES IN PRESCHOOL EDUCATION

Preschool education forms the bedrock of a child's long-term academic and personal growth, focusing on holistic development rather than solely on academic skills. Understanding the key learning objectives during this crucial stage is essential for educators and parents alike to ensure that children receive a well-rounded and enriching early education.

Social and Emotional Development

One of the primary objectives in preschool education is nurturing social and emotional development. This encompasses skills such as recognizing and managing one's own emotions, understanding and empathizing with others, forming positive relationships, and handling interpersonal situations effectively. Activities like group play, story time, and collaborative tasks help children develop these skills. For instance, a simple activity like a group circle time, where children talk about their feelings or share stories, can significantly boost their emotional intelligence and social skills.

Language and Communication Skills

Language and communication skills at this stage go beyond mere vocabulary building. The objective is to cultivate the ability to effectively express thoughts, understand others, and engage in meaningful communication. This includes listening skills, understanding non-verbal cues, and the ability to articulate ideas clearly. Interactive storytelling, singing, and engaging in conversations during playtime are practical ways to enhance these skills. For example, using picture books to tell a story allows children to connect words with images and emotions, thus enriching their language and communication skills.

Basic Literacy and Numeracy

While literacy and numeracy skills are often associated with primary education, laying the foundation in preschool is crucial. Basic literacy encompasses letter recognition, phonetic awareness, and beginning to understand written language. Numeracy includes understanding numbers, basic counting, and recognizing patterns. Games like "LeapFrog's Number Lovin' Oven" teach basic counting and number recognition in an interactive and fun way, making these concepts more relatable and understandable for young children.

Creativity and Expression

Fostering creativity and expression is a significant objective in preschool education. This involves encouraging imagination, artistic skills, and the ability to express thoughts and ideas creatively. Activities like drawing, painting, crafting, and dramatic play are instrumental in achieving this objective. For example, a simple activity like finger painting allows children to express their creativity while enhancing their fine motor skills.

Physical Development

Physical development in preschoolers focuses on both gross motor skills (like jumping, running, and balancing) and fine motor skills (such as holding a pencil, cutting with scissors, and manipulating small objects). These skills are crucial for everyday tasks and further academic activities. Incorporating physical activities like obstacle courses, dance, or even interactive digital games that require physical movement can significantly contribute to a child's physical development. A game like "GoNoodle" offers a range of movement and mindfulness videos that encourage kids to get active, promoting both physical health and mental well-being.

In summary, the key learning objectives in preschool education are multifaceted, encompassing social-emotional skills, language and communication, basic literacy and numeracy, creativity and expression, and physical development. These objectives work synergistically to support the overall growth of a child, setting a strong foundation for their future learning journey. By integrating various activities and interactive experiences, educators can effectively nurture these fundamental skills in preschoolers.

6

IMPORTANCE OF PLAY-BASED LEARNING IN EARLY CHILDHOOD

Play-based learning is fundamental in early childhood education, serving as a vital means through which young children gain a multitude of skills. This approach leverages the intrinsic nature of children, who are inherently curious and learn most effectively when they are active and enjoying themselves. Play-based learning encompasses a variety of activities that allow children to explore, discover, and make sense of the world around them.

Exploring the World Through Play

Play-based learning enables children to explore and interact with their environment in a natural and engaging way. This exploration is critical for cognitive development as it allows children to experiment, think creatively, and solve problems. For example, building blocks or construction play sets allow children to experiment with design and structure, enhancing their spatial awareness and problem-solving skills.

Understanding Social Dynamics

Play is a social activity and is crucial in helping children understand and navigate social dynamics. Through play, children learn to cooperate, share, negotiate, and resolve conflicts. Group games, whether they are structured or unstructured, provide opportunities for children to interact with peers, develop friendships, and learn the value of teamwork and collaboration.

Language Skills Development

Play-based learning also significantly contributes to language development. As children play, they communicate with each other, which enhances their vocabulary and improves their communication skills. Storytelling and role-playing games are particularly effective in this area. For instance, when children engage in pretend play, they often imitate adults and create dialogues, which helps in developing their language and storytelling skills.

Problem-Solving Through Play

Children engage in problem-solving naturally during play. They learn to think critically, make decisions, and develop a sense of curiosity and inquiry. Puzzles and strategy games, for example, require children to think logically and creatively to find solutions, fostering critical thinking skills that are essential for their future academic endeavors.

The Impact of Play on Future Academic and Social Challenges

Research indicates that children who have rich play-based learning experiences in their early years are better equipped to handle academic and social challenges in the future. Play nurtures a wide range of skills essential for success in school and beyond, including self-regulation, empathy, creativity, and cognitive flexibility.

Play-based learning is not just about physical play but also includes activities like drawing, storytelling, and music, which encourage children to express themselves and explore their creativity. For instance, a simple activity like drawing can help children express their emotions and develop fine motor skills, which are crucial for writing.

In conclusion, play-based learning is an integral part of early childhood education. It supports holistic development by aligning with the natural learning tendencies of children. Through play, children develop crucial cognitive, social, emotional, and physical skills. It is through this enjoyable and engaging process that they lay the foundations for a lifetime of learning and development. The role of educators and parents in facilitating and guiding play-based learning is essential to maximize its benefits and ensure children are prepared for future academic and social challenges.

7

HOW DIGITAL GAMES CAN SUPPORT THE ACHIEVEMENT OF LEARNING OBJECTIVES

Digital games, when integrated thoughtfully into preschool education, can be powerful tools in supporting the achievement of various learning objectives. These games are not only appealing to children but can also be tailored to target specific developmental skills such as numeracy, literacy, social-emotional skills, and more.

Enhancing Numeracy Skills

Digital games designed for numeracy can make learning numbers and basic mathematics more engaging and interactive. For instance, games like "Moose Math" by Duck Duck Moose offer a playful environment where children can learn counting, addition, subtraction, and geometry through fun activities. Such games often use colorful graphics, exciting characters, and engaging narratives to keep children interested, turning abstract concepts like numbers and shapes into tangible, interactive elements.

Supporting Literacy Development

In terms of literacy, digital games can significantly aid in teaching letters, phonics, and basic reading skills. Games like "ABCmouse" provide a series of activities that cover the alphabet, word recognition, and early reading. Through interactive storytelling and character-based challenges, these games make learning to read a fun and dynamic experience. The use of sounds, visuals, and interactive tasks in these games helps reinforce letter recognition and phonetic sounds, making them more memorable for young learners.

Fostering Social-Emotional Skills

Digital games are also effective tools for developing social-emotional skills. Games that simulate social situations or involve characters with varying emotions can teach children about empathy, cooperation, and emotional regulation. For example, "Daniel Tiger's

Neighborhood" games offer scenarios where children help characters navigate through social situations, learning about sharing, patience, and understanding others' feelings.

Adaptive Learning Technologies

One of the significant advantages of digital games in education is their ability to adapt to a child's individual learning pace. Many educational games come equipped with adaptive learning technologies, which adjust the difficulty level of tasks based on the child's performance. This feature ensures that children are neither bored with tasks that are too easy nor frustrated with overly challenging ones. For instance, a game might start with simple counting and gradually introduce larger numbers or basic arithmetic as the child demonstrates readiness.

Interactive and Engaging Learning Experience

The interactive nature of digital games can help solidify learning experiences in a way that traditional methods may not always achieve. Interactivity in learning through games ensures active participation, which is crucial for memory retention and understanding. For example, dragging and dropping items for counting or matching letters to sounds in a game involve active engagement that reinforces learning.

In conclusion, digital games, when used judiciously, can be instrumental in achieving preschool learning objectives. They offer an engaging, interactive, and often personalized learning experience that can make educational concepts more accessible and enjoyable for young children. By targeting specific developmental areas such as numeracy, literacy, and social-emotional skills, digital games can complement traditional teaching methods, making them a valuable asset in early childhood education.

8

ALIGNING DIGITAL GAMES WITH SPECIFIC LEARNING GOALS

Incorporating digital games into preschool education requires careful consideration to ensure they align with and support specific learning goals. By choosing games that are purposefully designed to develop particular skills or knowledge areas, educators can make the most of the educational potential these games offer.

Selecting Skill-Specific Games

The first step in aligning digital games with learning objectives is to select games that are explicitly designed for educational purposes. For example, for literacy objectives, educators might choose games like "Starfall ABCs," which focuses on phonetics and letter recognition. This game introduces children to the alphabet through songs, animations, and interactive activities that make learning letters engaging and effective.

For numeracy goals, a game like "Monkey Preschool Lunchbox" teaches counting, matching, and pattern recognition through a series of fun, food-themed mini-games. Such games make abstract concepts like numbers and patterns tangible and enjoyable for young learners.

Assessing Educational Content

Educators need to critically assess the educational content of digital games. This involves evaluating whether the game's content aligns with educational standards and learning objectives. The assessment can be based on how well the game introduces new concepts, reinforces existing knowledge, and encourages the application of skills.

For instance, a game designed for developing fine motor skills should have activities that require precise movements, like dragging items to specific locations or tracing shapes. "Dexteria Dots - Get in Touch with Math" is a game that combines fine motor skill development with basic math concepts, making it a suitable choice for multiple learning objectives.

Consulting Educational Standards

Aligning digital games with learning goals can be more effective when educators consult established educational standards or frameworks. These standards provide a guideline for what children at different developmental stages should know and be able to do. Matching games with these standards ensures that they are developmentally appropriate and meet the educational needs of the children.

For example, if a standard states that preschoolers should be able to recognize and name common shapes, a game like "Shapes Toddler Preschool" can be selected to reinforce this learning goal.

Incorporating Games into the Curriculum

Once suitable games have been selected, the next step is to integrate them into the curriculum effectively. This means not only allocating time for digital game play but also connecting the content of the games to other learning activities. For example, after playing a game that teaches shapes, educators might organize a hands-on activity where children create art using the shapes they learned.

Continuous Evaluation and Adjustment

Finally, the effectiveness of the games in achieving learning goals should be continuously evaluated. Educators should observe children's interactions with the games and assess their learning progress. If a game is not meeting the intended objectives, it may need to be replaced with one that is more suitable.

Aligning digital games with specific learning goals is a critical process in preschool education. It involves selecting the right games, assessing their educational content, consulting educational standards, integrating them into the curriculum, and continuously evaluating their effectiveness. By following these steps, educators can ensure that digital games are not just a source of entertainment but a valuable tool in achieving developmental milestones and learning objectives.

9

STRATEGIES FOR INTEGRATING DIGITAL GAMES INTO THE CURRICULUM

The integration of digital games into the preschool curriculum is a delicate balance that, when done correctly, can significantly enrich the learning experience. This process requires careful planning, clear objectives, and continuous monitoring to ensure that the digital games are effectively contributing to the educational development of the children.

Blending Digital Games with Traditional Learning

One effective strategy is to blend digital games with traditional teaching methods. This approach allows children to experience the best of both worlds – the engaging nature of digital games and the tactile, hands-on experience of traditional activities. For example, after a session with a counting game like "TallyTots Counting," children can reinforce what they've learned by engaging in a physical counting activity using blocks or beads. This helps solidify the concepts learned in the game through practical application.

Setting Clear Objectives for Game Use

Educators should have a clear understanding of what each game teaches and how it aligns with the curriculum's learning goals. This involves selecting games based on their educational content and how they can meet specific objectives. For instance, a game like "LetterSchool - Learn to Write!" can be chosen specifically to help children develop their letter formation skills, contributing to literacy objectives.

Monitoring and Adjusting Game Use

Continuous observation and assessment of how children interact with digital games are crucial. This monitoring helps educators assess the effectiveness of the games and make necessary adjustments. If a child is finding a game too challenging or too easy, the educator can modify the game's settings or choose a more appropriate game. This adaptive approach ensures that each child is engaged and learning at an appropriate level.

Incorporating Collaborative Play

Many digital games offer features that promote collaborative play. Incorporating these games into the curriculum can enhance social skills and teamwork. A game like "Toontastic 3D," which allows children to create stories and animations, can be used in a group setting where children collaborate to develop a story, thus encouraging teamwork and creative thinking.

Parental Involvement

Involving parents in the learning process is another important strategy. Educators can inform parents about the educational value of the games and suggest ways to extend learning at home. This can be done through regular communication, such as newsletters or parent-teacher meetings, where educators can share insights on effective educational games and how they complement the curriculum.

For example, parents can be encouraged to play a game like "Bugs and Numbers," which covers a range of math concepts, with their children at home, thus reinforcing the learning in a family setting.

Integrating digital games into the preschool curriculum is a multifaceted process that, when done strategically, can significantly enhance early education. By blending digital games with traditional learning, setting clear objectives, monitoring game use, incorporating collaborative play, and involving parents, educators can create a dynamic and effective learning environment. This approach ensures that digital games are not just a form of entertainment but a valuable educational tool that supports and enriches the preschool curriculum.

Selecting and Evaluating Interactive Digital Games

In the vibrant and interactive world of preschool education, selecting and evaluating the right digital games is a crucial task that can significantly enhance the learning experience of young children. This introduction provides an overview of the key aspects and strategies involved in choosing and assessing interactive digital games, ensuring they are not only engaging but also educational and developmentally appropriate for preschoolers.

When selecting interactive digital games for preschoolers, it is essential to consider a range of criteria to ensure the games are of high quality and offer genuine educational value. These criteria encompass educational content, user engagement, ease of use, feedback and adaptability, and overall design quality. The educational content should be the primary focus, ensuring the game aligns with specific learning objectives like numeracy, literacy, or problem-solving skills. For example, games designed to teach basic math concepts can be both intuitive and engaging, making complex ideas accessible and fun for young learners.

User engagement and interactivity are also key components of a high-quality digital game. The game should captivate the child's interest and motivate them to continue playing and learning. This can be achieved through colorful graphics, interesting characters, and interactive challenges. Additionally, the ease of use is crucial, as the game should be navigable by preschoolers without constant adult supervision.

Evaluating the educational value of a digital game involves assessing how effectively it teaches and reinforces learning concepts. This can be done by observing children's engagement with the game, the skills they develop, and any improvements in related knowledge or abilities. The game should also align with the learning goals of the preschool curriculum, catering to the specific educational objectives set for the children.

Selecting age-appropriate games is another critical aspect, ensuring the content is suitable for the child's age and provides the right level of challenge. Games should also adapt to different skill levels, allowing children to progress at their own pace and ensuring that learning remains a stimulating and rewarding experience.

Exploring a variety of digital game types is beneficial in catering to different learning styles and objectives. This includes puzzle games, story-based games, creative games like drawing or music creation, and even physical activity games that encourage movement. It's important to select games that appeal to a range of learning styles, ensuring that all children have the opportunity to learn in a way that suits them best.

Lastly, utilizing online platforms and reviews, such as those from Common Sense Media, can be a valuable resource in finding and reviewing educational games. Recommendations from educational technology experts and fellow teachers who have experience in integrating digital games into preschool settings can also provide insightful guidance.

In conclusion, this introduction underscores the importance of careful selection and evaluation of interactive digital games in preschool education. By focusing on these key aspects and utilizing available resources, educators can ensure that the digital games they introduce into their classrooms offer meaningful, engaging, and developmentally appropriate learning experiences for young children.

10

CRITERIA FOR SELECTING HIGH-QUALITY INTERACTIVE DIGITAL GAMES

Selecting the right digital games for preschoolers is a critical process that requires careful consideration of various factors to ensure the games are not only engaging but also of high educational value. Below are key criteria to consider:

Educational Content

The educational content of the game is paramount. The game should align with specific learning objectives relevant to the preschool curriculum, such as numeracy, literacy, or problem-solving skills. It's essential that the game not only entertains but also educates.

- **Numeracy**: For instance, "DragonBox Numbers" is an excellent example of a game designed to teach basic math concepts. It uses a unique approach to help children understand numbers and basic arithmetic in a fun and intuitive way.

Literacy: A game like "Endless Alphabet" is ideal for literacy objectives. It engages children with word puzzles that teach vocabulary and spelling in an interactive manner.

User Engagement and Interactivity

Engagement and interactivity are crucial components of effective educational games. The game should be able to capture and maintain the child's interest through various means.

- **Graphics and Sound**: Games with vibrant graphics, appealing characters, and stimulating sounds are more likely to engage young children. For example, "Peekaboo Barn" uses colorful animations and fun sounds to keep children interested while they learn the names of various farm animals.

- **Interactive Challenges**: Games should also include interactive elements that keep children active and involved. For instance, "Toca Boca" games offer a variety of interactive scenarios where children can experiment and play creatively, keeping them engaged through active participation.

Ease of Use

The ease of use is especially important for young learners who are still developing their fine motor skills and cognitive abilities.

- **User-Friendly Interface**: The game should have a simple, intuitive interface that children can navigate independently. A game like "PBS Kids Play" offers a straightforward interface that allows children to explore various educational activities without needing constant help from an adult.

- **Simple Instructions**: Instructions within the game should be clear and easily understandable. Games that use visual cues or spoken instructions can be more accessible to preschoolers who may not yet be able to read.

Feedback and Adaptability

Feedback mechanisms and adaptability are also important factors in selecting digital games.

- **Immediate Feedback**: Games that provide immediate feedback, such as verbal praise or visual rewards when a task is completed correctly, can be very encouraging for young learners.

- **Adaptive Difficulty**: The game should be able to adapt to the child's skill level, providing a suitable level of challenge. Games with adjustable difficulty levels or that progressively become more challenging as the child's skills improve, like "Montessori Crosswords," are ideal as they grow with the child.

Design Quality

Lastly, the overall design quality of the game, including its aesthetic appeal, sound design, and the smoothness of its gameplay, is important.

- **Aesthetic Appeal**: The game should be visually appealing to children. Bright colors, fun characters, and engaging animations can make the game more attractive.

- **Smooth Gameplay**: The game should run smoothly without technical glitches, which can be frustrating for young children and can hinder the learning process.

In conclusion, selecting high-quality interactive digital games for preschoolers involves evaluating the educational content, user engagement and interactivity, ease of use, feedback mechanisms, adaptability, and overall design quality. Games that meet these criteria are likely to be more effective as educational tools and more enjoyable for young learners.

11

Evaluating the Educational Value of Digital Games

Determining the educational value of digital games in a preschool setting involves a multifaceted approach. This process ensures that the games are not only engaging and enjoyable but also effective as learning tools. Here are some strategies and considerations for evaluating the educational value of digital games:

Assessment Strategies

1. **Observing Children's Engagement**: The first step in evaluating a game's educational value is to observe how children interact with it. Are they engaged and focused while playing? Do they seem motivated to achieve the game's objectives? For example, in a game like "Bugs and Buttons," children are often visibly engaged in sorting, counting, and matching activities, indicating a high level of engagement.

2. **Assessing Skill Development**: It's crucial to evaluate the skills that children develop while playing. This involves looking at both the intended learning outcomes of the game and any additional skills that children might be acquiring. For instance, a game designed to teach counting may also inadvertently improve hand-eye coordination.

3. **Tracking Improvement in Knowledge and Abilities**: Monitor the children's progress in specific areas related to the game. For example, after playing a game like "Fish School HD," which focuses on basic shapes, colors, and numbers, educators should look for improvements in children's ability to identify these concepts during non-game activities.

Alignment with Learning Goals
1. **Curriculum Compatibility**: The game should be compatible with the preschool curriculum's learning goals. This alignment ensures that the game is reinforcing what is being taught in the classroom. For example, if the curriculum emphasizes early literacy, a game like "Endless Reader," which focuses on word recognition and phonics, would be suitable.

2. **Comprehensiveness**: Evaluate whether the game covers the breadth of the intended learning objective. It's important that the game is not too narrow in focus, but instead provides a comprehensive understanding of the topic. For example, a literacy game should ideally cover a range of skills from letter recognition to basic word formation.

3. **Age-Appropriate Content**: The content of the game should be appropriate for the age group it is intended for. This includes considering the complexity of the game's language, the nature of its challenges, and the type of feedback it provides. For younger preschoolers, games should have simpler tasks and more immediate and positive feedback.

4. **Feedback Mechanism**: The way a game provides feedback to children is crucial in their learning process. Positive reinforcement and constructive feedback can significantly enhance the learning experience. In a game like "Little Alchemy," for instance, children experiment with combining different elements to create new ones, receiving immediate feedback on their actions.

5. **Cultural and Contextual Relevance**: Evaluate whether the game is culturally and contextually relevant for the children playing it. This includes considering the game's language, characters, scenarios, and overall setting. Games that reflect a child's own experiences and environment can be more engaging and effective for learning.

In summary, evaluating the educational value of digital games in a preschool setting involves a combination of observing children's engagement and skill development, assessing improvement in knowledge and abilities, and ensuring alignment with the curriculum's learning goals. Games that meet these criteria are more likely to be beneficial as educational tools, contributing positively to the children's learning experience.

12

Considering Age-Appropriateness and Skill Levels in Game Selection

Selecting digital games for preschoolers requires a keen understanding of their developmental stages and abilities. Age-appropriateness and skill level considerations are paramount to ensure that the games not only engage children but also support their learning without causing undue frustration or boredom.

Age-Appropriate Content

1. **Tailoring to Developmental Stages**: It's essential to choose games that are tailored to the specific developmental stage of the children. For younger preschoolers (ages 3-4), games should focus on basic concepts like color and shape recognition, simple counting, and basic problem-solving. An example is "Peek-a-Zoo by Duck Duck Moose," which helps young children learn about animals, their sounds, and behaviors in an interactive setting.

2. **Increasing Complexity for Older Preschoolers**: For older preschoolers (ages 4-5), games can be more complex, introducing basic literacy and numeracy concepts, simple word puzzles, and more intricate problem-solving tasks. A game like "ABC Spelling - Spell & Phonics" is ideal for this age group as it introduces simple spelling and phonetic recognition through engaging puzzles.

3. **Catering to Diverse Learning Needs**: Consideration should also be given to the diverse learning needs within the same age group. A one-size-fits-all approach may not be effective, so selecting a range of games that cater to different skill levels and learning styles is important.

Skill-Level Appropriateness

1. **Evaluating Individual Abilities**: Assessing the individual abilities and skill levels of children is crucial in game selection. Some children may have advanced skills in certain areas, while others may require more foundational support. Games that offer multiple levels or adjustable difficulty settings can be beneficial in this regard.

2. **Progressive Difficulty Levels**: Games that progressively increase in difficulty are advantageous as they can adapt to a child's learning curve. For instance, "Endless Numbers" offers a range of levels from basic number recognition to more complex addition and subtraction, allowing children to progress at their own pace.

3. **Feedback and Adaptation**: Games that provide feedback and adapt to the child's responses can help educators and parents gauge whether the game is appropriately challenging. For example, a game that adjusts the difficulty based on the child's responses can ensure that they are neither overwhelmed nor under-challenged.

Practical Considerations

1. **Ease of Play**: The game's interface should be simple enough for the child to navigate independently. Games with too many controls or complicated instructions can be frustrating for younger children and may deter them from playing and learning.

2. **Safety and Privacy**: Safety and privacy are also important considerations, especially for digital games. Games should be free from inappropriate content, and personal data collection should be minimal and secure.

3. **Cultural Sensitivity**: Lastly, the cultural relevance and sensitivity of the game's content are important, especially in diverse classrooms. Games should be inclusive and represent a wide range of cultures and backgrounds.

In conclusion, considering age-appropriateness and skill levels in game selection is a nuanced process that involves understanding the developmental stages and individual abilities of preschoolers. By selecting games that provide the right level of challenge and engagement for each age group and skill level, educators and parents can create a supportive and effective learning environment through digital games.

13

Exploring Different Types of Digital Games for Preschoolers

Introducing a variety of digital game types in preschool education is essential to cater to diverse learning styles and developmental needs. By offering a range of games, educators can ensure that all children have the opportunity to engage in activities that resonate with their individual learning preferences.

Puzzle Games

- **Cognitive Development and Problem-Solving**: Puzzle games are excellent for cognitive development and problem-solving skills. They encourage children to think logically and develop strategies to overcome challenges. For preschoolers, simple jigsaw puzzles or matching games like "Memory" can be particularly beneficial. These games often involve matching pairs of cards, which helps to improve memory and concentration.

Story-Based Games

- **Language and Literacy Skills**: Story-based games are great for developing language and literacy skills. They typically involve narratives that children can follow along with, helping to develop listening skills and comprehension. "Toontastic 3D" is an example of a story-based game where children can create their own stories, enhancing their creativity and narrative skills.

Creative Games

- **Artistic Expression and Creativity**: Creative games, such as drawing or music creation apps, allow children to express themselves artistically. An app like "Drawing Pad" lets children draw, color, and create artwork, encouraging their artistic skills and imagination. Music games like "Toca Band" enable children to experiment with different sounds and rhythms, fostering an appreciation for music and rhythm.

Physical Activity Games
- **Physical Development and Coordination**: Games that involve physical movement are important for developing gross motor skills and coordination. Games that use motion control technology, such as "Dance Dance Revolution" or simple interactive dancing apps, encourage children to move their bodies and develop physical coordination and rhythm.

Incorporating Diverse Learning Styles
- **Visual Learners**: For visual learners, games with rich graphics and visual puzzles are particularly appealing. Games that involve sorting shapes or colors, like "Shape Sorting" apps, can be very effective.

- **Auditory Learners**: For children who are auditory learners, games with a strong emphasis on sounds, music, and spoken instructions can be more engaging. Storytelling apps with narrated stories or games with musical elements cater to these learners.

- **Kinesthetic Learners**: Kinesthetic learners benefit from games that involve physical activity or tactile interaction. Touch-based games or apps that require physical movement allow these children to learn through movement and touch.

Balancing Digital Game Types

It's important for educators to balance these different types of games to ensure a well-rounded learning experience. By incorporating a variety of game types into the curriculum, children are exposed to different ways of learning and can develop a broad range of skills.

Additionally, educators should periodically assess and adjust the selection of games to align with the changing interests and developmental stages of the children. This ensures that the games remain engaging and effective as educational tools.

In conclusion, exploring different types of digital games and incorporating them to cater to various learning styles can significantly enhance the learning experience in preschool settings. By carefully selecting and balancing these games, educators can provide an inclusive and dynamic learning environment that supports the development of a wide range of skills and caters to the diverse needs of all learners.

14

RESOURCES FOR FINDING AND REVIEWING INTERACTIVE DIGITAL GAMES

Incorporating digital games into preschool education requires careful selection to ensure their educational quality and suitability. Several resources, both online and through professional networks, can assist educators in finding and reviewing the best interactive digital games for their classrooms.

Utilizing Online Platforms and Reviews

1. **Educational Game Review Sites**: Websites dedicated to reviewing educational games can be invaluable resources. Common Sense Media is a notable example, offering detailed reviews and age recommendations for a wide range of digital games. Their reviews often include information about the educational aspects of the games, ease of use, and how engaging they are for children.

2. **Parent and Teacher Forums**: Online forums and communities for parents and educators can be excellent places to discover and discuss digital games. Platforms like Teachers Pay Teachers or Mumsnet often have sections where users share their experiences and recommendations regarding various educational resources, including digital games.

3. **Educational Technology Blogs and Websites**: Websites and blogs focusing on educational technology often review and suggest digital games that are beneficial for preschool learning. These websites might also provide guides on how to effectively integrate these games into the classroom.

4. **App Store Reviews**: For a quick assessment, the review sections on app stores like Google Play and Apple App Store can be helpful. These reviews, often

written by parents and educators, can give insights into the game's performance, engagement level, and educational value.

Professional Recommendations

1. **Educational Technology Experts**: Consulting with educational technology experts can provide valuable insights into the best digital games for preschoolers. These experts may have access to the latest research and can recommend games based on proven educational strategies.

2. **Fellow Educators**: Fellow teachers who have experience integrating digital games into their preschool curriculum can be excellent resources. They can share firsthand experiences about which games have been successful and offer tips on implementation.

3. **Professional Development Workshops**: Attending professional development workshops and seminars on early childhood education and technology can also provide opportunities to learn about effective digital games. These workshops often feature demonstrations of educational games and discussions on best practices for their use.

4. **Educational Conferences and Expos**: Educational conferences and expos are great places to learn about the newest and most effective digital games. These events often feature exhibitions from educational game developers, allowing educators to explore and test different games firsthand.

5. **Library and Educational Resource Centers**: Local libraries and educational resource centers sometimes have collections of digital learning tools, including games, that educators can explore. Librarians or resource center staff might also be able to recommend games that have been popular or well-received in the community.

In summary, a multitude of resources are available for educators seeking to find and review interactive digital games for preschoolers. Utilizing online platforms, seeking professional recommendations, participating in workshops and conferences, and exploring local educational resources can greatly assist in the selection of high-quality, appropriate digital games. By tapping into these resources, educators can make informed decisions that enrich the learning experience for their preschool students.

Designing Effective Learning Experiences with Digital Games

The integration of digital games in preschool education opens a new frontier in designing effective learning experiences for young learners. This introduction sets the stage for an in-depth exploration of how digital games can be crafted and utilized to create enriching and educational experiences that captivate and motivate preschool-aged children.

At the heart of effective game-based learning design lie foundational principles that ensure these digital tools are not just entertaining but also educational. Key to this is aligning games with educational objectives, crafting immersive and interactive experiences, and ensuring a balance between challenge and skill level. This introduction will delve into how these principles are crucial in creating games that engage young minds while simultaneously fostering their learning.

A significant aspect of game design for preschoolers is the focus on engagement and motivation. Elements such as compelling storylines, relatable characters, appropriate rewards, and age-suitable challenges are essential. These aspects help in making the games appealing and keeping young learners invested in the learning process.

Beyond the design of the games themselves, this introduction will explore strategies for integrating digital games into lesson plans and classroom activities. It will provide insights on selecting games that complement specific learning goals and how these games can be part of a broader educational strategy, offering practical examples across various subject areas like literacy, math, science, and social studies.

Interactivity is a cornerstone of engaging learning experiences in digital games. This section will discuss maximizing the interactivity of digital games, emphasizing hands-on activities, exploration, and experimentation. Additionally, guidance on selecting games that offer interactive and engaging experiences will be provided, focusing on criteria such as user control, activity variety, and creative elements.

A crucial component of game-based learning is incorporating assessment and feedback mechanisms. This introduction will examine how games can serve as tools for assessing student progress and understanding, featuring in-game quizzes, challenges, and feedback mechanisms. The importance of immediate and constructive feedback will be highlighted, showcasing how it can foster resilience and a growth mindset among young learners.

Adapting games to meet individual student needs is another key focus. This includes personalization techniques like adjustable difficulty levels and personalized learning paths, ensuring games cater to the diverse learning paces and styles of each child. Strategies for supporting diverse learners, including those with disabilities or needing additional support, will be discussed.

Finally, this introduction will present case studies and real-world examples of effective game-based learning. These examples will illuminate how digital games have been successfully implemented in preschool settings and their impact on learning outcomes. Lessons learned and best practices from these real-world applications will provide valuable insights into what works well in game-based learning and common pitfalls to avoid.

In conclusion, designing effective learning experiences with digital games in preschool education is a multifaceted process that requires a deep understanding of educational principles, child psychology, and technological innovation. This introduction aims to equip educators and developers with the knowledge and strategies needed to effectively harness the power of digital games in creating meaningful and impactful learning experiences for young children.

15

Principles of Effective Game-Based Learning Design

Designing effective game-based learning experiences for preschoolers requires an understanding of several foundational principles. These principles ensure that the games are not only fun and engaging but also serve a clear educational purpose.

Foundational Principles

1. **Alignment with Educational Objectives**: The most crucial principle is aligning the game with specific educational objectives. This means that the game's design should directly support the learning goals, whether they are related to literacy, numeracy, problem-solving, or social-emotional skills. For example, a game designed to teach counting should have clear, engaging activities specifically focused on number recognition and counting skills.

2. **Creating Immersive and Interactive Experiences**: Immersion and interactivity are key to capturing and sustaining children's attention. An immersive game typically has a well-thought-out storyline or context, which can be as simple as a virtual journey or a quest for treasure. The goal is to create an environment where learning objectives are woven into the narrative, making the educational aspect a natural part of the gameplay.

3. **Balancing Challenge with Skill Level**: Games should be challenging enough to keep children engaged but not so difficult that they become frustrating. This balance is crucial in game-based learning design. For younger preschoolers, games might involve simple matching or sorting tasks, while for older preschoolers, the games might include more complex puzzles. The idea is to progressively challenge children in a way that aligns with their developmental stages.

Engagement and Motivation
1. **Storylines and Characters**: Engaging storylines and relatable characters can greatly enhance a child's interest in a game. Characters that preschoolers can empathize with, like animals or friendly fictional characters, add a personal touch to the game. For instance, a game featuring a character on a quest to find hidden letters or numbers can make the process of learning these concepts more exciting and relatable.

2. **Rewards and Incentives**: Appropriate rewards and incentives are powerful tools in maintaining engagement. These could be in-game rewards like points, badges, or unlocking new levels or characters. The key is to provide positive reinforcement for educational achievements within the game.

3. **Age-Appropriate Challenges**: Challenges within the game should be age-appropriate and achievable. For preschoolers, these could be simple tasks like identifying colors, shapes, or simple words. The challenges should gradually increase in complexity as the child's skills develop.

4. **Interactive Elements**: Games that require active participation, like touching, dragging, or speaking into the device, can enhance engagement. Interactive elements make the game experience more dynamic and hands-on, which is particularly effective for young learners.

Visual and Audio Elements: The use of vibrant colors, appealing graphics, and cheerful audio can significantly enhance a game's engagement factor. Sounds like music, character voices, and sound effects can make the game more enjoyable and reinforce the learning process.

In conclusion, designing effective game-based learning experiences for preschoolers involves a careful balance of educational content, engagement strategies, and age-appropriate challenges. By adhering to these foundational principles, educators and game developers can create digital games that are not only fun but also serve as valuable educational tools.

16

INTEGRATING DIGITAL GAMES INTO LESSON PLANS AND ACTIVITIES

Incorporating digital games into preschool education requires strategic planning and thoughtful integration. This ensures that the games enhance the learning experience and complement traditional teaching methods. Below are strategies and practical examples of how digital games can be integrated into various subject areas.

Strategic Integration

1. **Aligning Games with Learning Objectives**: The first step in integration is selecting games that align with the specific learning objectives of your lesson plan. For instance, if the objective is to improve number recognition, a game like "Counting Caterpillar" would be appropriate.

2. **Blending with Traditional Methods**: Digital games should be used in conjunction with traditional teaching methods. For example, after using a digital storytelling game, teachers can encourage students to draw scenes from the story or engage in a group discussion about the story's themes.

3. **Timing and Frequency**: Consider the timing and frequency of game use. Games can be used as an introductory activity to pique interest, a mid-lesson interactive break, or a concluding activity to reinforce concepts.

4. **Facilitating Game-Based Learning**: Teachers play a crucial role in guiding and facilitating game-based learning. This involves setting up the game, explaining the objectives, and helping children navigate the game if needed.

Practical Examples

1. **Literacy**: In a literacy lesson focusing on phonics, a game like "Starfall Learn to

Read" can be used. This game offers interactive activities that teach letter sounds and reading. Post-game activities can include a phonics scavenger hunt where children find objects that start with a specific letter sound.

2. **Math**: For a math lesson on basic counting and addition, a game like "Moose Math" can engage students. After the game session, a hands-on activity like counting physical objects or using addition flashcards can reinforce the concepts learned in the game.

3. **Science**: In a science lesson about plant life cycles, a game like "Grow a Plant" can be an effective interactive tool. Following the game, children can plant seeds in the classroom and observe their growth over time, relating it back to the game.

4. **Social Studies**: For teaching about community helpers, a game like "Little Fire Station" allows children to explore different roles. After playing, a role-playing activity where children pretend to be different community helpers can consolidate their understanding.

5. **Art and Creativity**: Digital drawing games or apps like "Toca Art Lab" can be integrated into art lessons. Children can first create digital art and then replicate their creations using physical art materials.

6. **Physical Education**: Games that involve physical movement, like "GoNoodle," can be integrated into physical education lessons to encourage active play and teach coordination and rhythm.

Integrating digital games into lesson plans and classroom activities requires careful planning and execution. By strategically choosing games that align with learning objectives and blending them with traditional teaching methods, educators can create a dynamic and engaging learning environment. These digital games can effectively complement lessons in literacy, math, science, social studies, art, and physical education, making learning a more interactive and enjoyable experience for preschoolers.

17

CREATING INTERACTIVE AND ENGAGING LEARNING EXPERIENCES WITH GAMES

To harness the full potential of digital games in preschool education, it's essential to create learning experiences that are both interactive and engaging. This involves careful consideration of the game's design and how it is used in the classroom.

Maximizing Interactivity

1. **Hands-On Activities**: Integrating hands-on activities with digital gaming enhances learning. For example, after playing a digital game about shapes, children can engage in a physical activity where they create shapes using clay or building blocks. This combination of digital and physical interaction reinforces learning and keeps children engaged.

2. **Exploration and Experimentation**: Games that encourage exploration and experimentation allow children to learn through discovery. For instance, a game like "Toca Nature" lets children create and explore their own virtual forests, mountains, and rivers, learning about nature in a free and exploratory way.

3. **Incorporating Real-World Elements**: Games that incorporate real-world elements or mimic real-life scenarios can make learning more relatable and engaging. For example, a cooking game where children follow recipes can teach them about measurements, following instructions, and the concept of time.

Game Selection

1. **User Control**: Games that offer a high level of user control are more engaging. Look for games that allow children to make choices, such as selecting characters or deciding what path to take in a story. This not only makes the game more

engaging but also fosters decision-making skills.

2. **Variety of Activities**: Games with a variety of activities cater to different interests and learning styles. For example, "ABCya!" offers a range of educational games covering topics from math to art, providing diverse learning experiences within one platform.

3. **Creative Elements**: Games that include creative elements, such as drawing, music composition, or building, encourage creativity and self-expression. A game like "Artie's World," where children draw paths and shapes to navigate through a story, can stimulate creativity and problem-solving skills.

4. **Social Interaction**: Games that allow for social interaction, either through multiplayer features or by encouraging group play in the classroom, can enhance social skills. For instance, games that involve turn-taking or cooperative tasks can be used to teach the importance of teamwork and communication.

5. **Adaptability and Customization**: Games that offer adaptability and customization options can be tailored to fit the needs and skill levels of different children. This ensures that all children, regardless of their abilities, can participate and benefit from the game.

6. **Feedback and Progress Tracking**: Select games that provide feedback and allow progress tracking. This helps educators and parents understand how the child is interacting with the game and what skills they are developing.

In conclusion, creating interactive and engaging learning experiences with digital games involves a combination of maximizing interactivity through hands-on activities and thoughtful game selection. By focusing on user control, the variety of activities, creative elements, social interaction, adaptability, and feedback mechanisms, educators can select games that not only captivate children's interest but also significantly enhance their learning experience.

18

INCORPORATING ASSESSMENT AND FEEDBACK MECHANISMS IN GAME DESIGN

Assessment and feedback mechanisms are critical components of educational game design. These features not only monitor and support student progress but also enhance the learning experience by providing immediate, personalized feedback.

Assessment Tools in Game-Based Learning

1. **In-Game Quizzes and Challenges**: Many educational games incorporate quizzes and challenges as a fun way to assess understanding. These can range from simple recall questions to complex problem-solving tasks. For example, a game like "Math Blaster" uses math challenges as part of its space adventure theme, allowing children to apply mathematical concepts in a game setting.

2. **Progress Tracking Features**: Games with progress tracking give teachers and parents insight into a child's learning journey. These features can often show which areas a child excels in and where they may need more practice. For instance, "Reading Eggs" includes a progress dashboard that displays the child's achievements and areas to focus on.

3. **Adaptive Learning Algorithms**: Some games use adaptive learning algorithms that adjust the difficulty of tasks based on the child's performance. This ensures that the game remains challenging but not beyond the child's capabilities. "DreamBox Learning Math" is an example of a game that adapts in real time to the learner's responses.

Feedback for Learning
1. **Immediate Feedback**: Immediate feedback in games can reinforce correct answers and help children learn from mistakes. This can be as simple as positive sound effects for correct answers or gentle redirection for incorrect ones. For example, a game like "LeapFrog Academy" provides encouraging auditory feedback that rewards correct answers and offers hints when a child struggles.

2. **Constructive Feedback**: Constructive feedback is key to helping children understand what they did wrong and how to improve. Digital games designed for learning should include feedback that is specific, informative, and leads to an improved understanding of the concept.

3. **Encouraging Persistence and Resilience**: Feedback should be designed to encourage persistence and resilience. For example, rather than simply indicating a wrong answer, a game could provide a message like "Try again, you're getting closer!" or "Think about what you did last time, and try a different approach!"

4. **Promoting a Growth Mindset**: The way feedback is presented can influence a child's mindset about learning. Feedback should be structured in a way that promotes a growth mindset, emphasizing that abilities can be developed through dedication and hard work. Games like "The Foos" encourage this by celebrating the effort and strategy rather than just the outcome.

Incorporating assessment and feedback mechanisms in game design is crucial for creating effective educational games. These elements not only assess and support student learning but also enhance the educational value of the game through immediate, personalized, and constructive feedback. By leveraging these tools, educational games can help foster a positive learning environment where children are motivated to learn and grow.

19

ADAPTING GAMES TO MEET INDIVIDUAL STUDENT NEEDS

Adapting digital games to meet the individual needs of preschoolers is crucial in creating an inclusive and effective learning environment. By employing various personalization techniques and strategies, games can cater to a wide range of learning styles, abilities, and paces.

Personalization Techniques

1. **Adjustable Difficulty Levels**: Offering adjustable difficulty levels in games ensures that they are accessible and challenging for children with different skill levels. For example, a literacy game might start with simple letter recognition for beginners and progress to word formation for more advanced learners. A game like "ABC Mouse" offers activities that vary in difficulty, catering to a range of learning levels.

2. **Choice of Activities**: Allowing children to choose from a variety of activities within a game can cater to their interests and learning preferences. This choice can motivate children to engage more deeply with the content. In a game like "Busy Shapes," children can choose different types of puzzle activities, which helps maintain their interest and engagement.

3. **Personalized Learning Paths**: Some games offer personalized learning paths that adapt based on the child's interactions and progress. This can include recommending specific activities to strengthen certain skills or providing additional challenges in areas where the child excels. For instance, "AdaptedMind" creates customized math and reading practice that adjusts to each child's level.

Supporting Diverse Learners
1. **Learners with Disabilities**: For children with disabilities, games with customizable settings can be beneficial. For example, games with options to change text size, add subtitles, or modify color contrasts can help children with visual impairments. Audio-based games or games with minimal reliance on fine motor skills can support children with physical disabilities.

2. **Advanced Learners**: For advanced learners, games that offer deeper levels of complexity or open-ended challenges can provide the necessary stimulation and keep them engaged. Games that encourage problem-solving and critical thinking, such as "Lightbot: Code Hour," challenge advanced learners with basic coding puzzles.

3. **Learners Needing Additional Support**: For children who need more support, games with repetitive practice and incremental challenges can be effective. These games should offer a supportive and non-penalizing environment where children can learn at their own pace without fear of making mistakes. A game like "Endless Alphabet" is beneficial for its repetitive yet engaging approach to learning the alphabet and vocabulary.

4. **Culturally Inclusive Games**: It's also important to select games that are culturally inclusive and represent a diverse range of backgrounds and experiences. This helps all children feel represented and valued.

Adapting digital games to meet individual student needs is a key aspect of effective game-based learning in preschool settings. By employing personalization techniques and supporting diverse learners, educators can ensure that each child receives an educational experience that is tailored to their unique needs and abilities. This approach not only enhances learning outcomes but also fosters an inclusive and supportive learning environment.

Supporting Social and Emotional Development through Digital Games

The introduction of digital games in preschool education offers a unique and powerful avenue for supporting social and emotional development in young learners. This introduction sets the stage for an insightful exploration of how digital games can be leveraged to enhance and cultivate crucial social and emotional skills in preschoolers.

Social and emotional learning (SEL) forms the cornerstone of early childhood development, laying the foundation for how children build relationships, manage emotions, and navigate social environments. The importance of these skills cannot be overstated, as they significantly contribute to a child's long-term development, impacting academic performance, mental health, and the ability to form successful interpersonal relationships.

Digital games present a unique opportunity to enhance social and emotional development in children. They offer interactive learning opportunities where children can engage in simulated social scenarios and emotional challenges within a controlled, safe environment. This section will delve into how these games can be structured to facilitate the acquisition and practice of social and emotional skills.

The use of narrative and characters in digital games is a powerful tool for teaching empathy and understanding emotions. Games with storylines that require players to interpret and respond to characters' emotions can be particularly effective in fostering empathy and social understanding. Additionally, role-playing games allow children to step into different perspectives, enhancing their ability to empathize and appreciate diverse viewpoints.

Cooperative digital games can also play a significant role in developing teamwork skills. By requiring children to collaborate to achieve common goals, these games teach valuable lessons in cooperation, sharing, and collective problem-solving. Furthermore, games that incorporate scenarios requiring conflict resolution can impart essential skills in managing disagreements and fostering peace.

Beyond social skills, digital games can also promote emotional expression and self-regulation. Games that help children recognize and express their emotions contribute to emotional awareness. Similarly, games that involve overcoming challenges teach self-regulation skills, such as patience, perseverance, and managing frustration.

To further enhance the social aspect of game-based learning, strategies for fostering multiplayer interactions and blending digital with real-world socialization will be discussed. This includes selecting games that encourage communication and teamwork, as well as extending game experiences into real-world activities that promote collaboration and shared experiences among children.

Lastly, the role of educators in facilitating social learning through digital games is crucial. Educators can guide and enhance the learning experience, using games as teachable moments for social and emotional development. This section will highlight how teachers can effectively use digital games as tools for fostering social interaction and emotional growth in preschool settings.

In conclusion, this introduction paves the way for a comprehensive understanding of how digital games can be effectively utilized in preschool education to support and enrich the social and emotional development of young learners. By carefully selecting and implementing these digital tools, educators can provide children with engaging and meaningful experiences that build essential life skills.

20

UNDERSTANDING THE IMPORTANCE OF SOCIAL AND EMOTIONAL SKILLS IN PRESCHOOL

In the tender years of early childhood, the foundation of social and emotional learning (SEL) is laid, shaping preschoolers into individuals capable of understanding emotions, forging positive relationships, and navigating the complex tapestry of social interactions.

Foundation of Social and Emotional Learning

Social and emotional learning (SEL) in early childhood is pivotal for the holistic development of preschoolers. This learning aspect encompasses the skills necessary for children to understand and manage emotions, feel and show empathy for others, establish positive relationships, and make responsible decisions.

1. **Building Relationships**: Social and emotional skills lay the groundwork for how children interact with others. These skills help children understand social cues, share with their peers, and develop friendships. The ability to form healthy relationships in these early years is crucial for their social development.

2. **Managing Emotions**: Preschoolers are at a stage where they begin to experience a wide range of emotions. SEL helps them recognize and understand these emotions, express them appropriately, and regulate their feelings. This emotional management is key to their well-being and ability to cope with challenges.

3. **Navigating Social Environments**: Effective social and emotional skills enable children to navigate various social environments, from interacting with peers in the playground to responding to adults in structured settings. These skills are essential for adapting to different social norms and expectations.

Impact on Long-Term Development

The development of social and emotional skills in preschool has a profound and lasting impact on children's lives.

1. **Improved Academic Performance**: Children with strong SEL skills tend to perform better academically. Skills like self-regulation, attention, and cooperation are closely linked to success in school. For example, a child who can regulate emotions is better able to focus in class and tackle academic tasks effectively.

2. **Better Mental Health**: Early development of SEL skills is linked to better mental health outcomes. Children who can manage their emotions and build strong relationships are less likely to experience mental health issues like anxiety and depression. This emotional resilience is crucial in coping with life's challenges.

3. **Successful Interpersonal Relationships**: SEL skills are the foundation for building successful interpersonal relationships throughout life. The ability to empathize with others, communicate effectively, and resolve conflicts amicably are vital for personal and professional relationships.

4. **Career Success**: In the long term, SEL skills contribute to career success. Many employers now recognize the importance of skills like teamwork, communication, and emotional intelligence in the workplace. Children who develop these skills early are well-placed to succeed in their future careers.

In summary, the development of social and emotional skills during the preschool years is foundational for children's immediate well-being and their long-term academic, mental, and interpersonal success. Fostering these skills through structured learning experiences, including digital games, is an investment in children's futures, equipping them with the necessary tools to navigate life's challenges and opportunities.

21

HOW DIGITAL GAMES CAN ENHANCE SOCIAL AND EMOTIONAL DEVELOPMENT

In the intersection of technology and child development, digital games emerge as powerful tools in nurturing the social and emotional growth of young learners.

Interactive Learning Opportunities

Digital games offer unique interactive opportunities that can significantly enhance the social and emotional development of preschool children. These interactive experiences can effectively simulate real-life scenarios, providing a safe and controlled environment for children to learn and practice essential social and emotional skills.

1. **Simulating Social Scenarios**: Many digital games create virtual environments that mimic real-life social situations. For example, games where children play roles in a virtual community, like a digital playground or classroom, can teach them about sharing, cooperation, and understanding social norms. They learn to navigate these scenarios, make decisions, and see the consequences of their actions in a risk-free setting.

2. **Emotional Challenges**: Games can also present challenges that require children to recognize and manage emotions. For instance, a game that involves caring for a virtual pet or character can teach empathy and responsibility. Children learn to respond to the character's needs, understanding feelings like happiness, sadness, or frustration, and how their actions affect others.

3. **Problem-Solving in Social Contexts**: Many games incorporate problem-solving within a social context, teaching children to think critically about how their decisions impact others. These games often involve scenarios where players must work together to solve puzzles or overcome obstacles, promoting teamwork and

communication.

Role of Narrative and Characters

Narratives and characters in digital games play a vital role in teaching social and emotional skills. Engaging stories and relatable characters can be powerful tools for fostering empathy, understanding emotions, and enhancing social interactions.

1. **Empathy through Storytelling**: Games with strong narratives allow children to immerse themselves in the stories of different characters, helping them to understand and empathize with varied experiences and emotions. For example, a game with a storyline involving characters from diverse backgrounds can teach children about empathy and inclusivity.

2. **Characters as Emotional Models**: Characters in games can also serve as models for expressing and managing emotions. Games that feature characters displaying a range of emotions in different situations can help children learn to identify and articulate their feelings.

3. **Interactive Story-Based Learning**: Interactive story-based games where children make decisions that influence the narrative can be particularly effective in teaching social and emotional skills. These games often require children to consider the feelings and perspectives of characters before making decisions, thereby enhancing their emotional intelligence and decision-making skills.

4. **Enhancing Social Understanding**: Games that involve character interactions, dialogues, and social problem-solving can enhance children's understanding of social dynamics. They learn about cooperation, conflict resolution, and the importance of understanding and respecting different perspectives.

In conclusion, digital games can significantly contribute to the social and emotional development of preschoolers. By providing interactive learning opportunities and utilizing narrative and characters effectively, these games can teach important social and emotional skills in an engaging and impactful way. The controlled and safe environment of digital games allows children to experiment with social interactions and emotional responses, preparing them for real-world experiences.

22

ADDRESSING EMPATHY, COOPERATION, AND CONFLICT RESOLUTION THROUGH GAMES

Digital games can play a significant role in teaching preschool children valuable social skills such as empathy, cooperation, and conflict resolution. These skills are essential for their social and emotional development and future interactions.

Empathy Building through Role-Playing

Role-playing games (RPGs) offer unique opportunities for children to step into different roles, which can be instrumental in developing empathy and understanding.

1. **Understanding Different Perspectives**: RPGs often involve scenarios where children assume the roles of different characters, each with their own stories and challenges. For example, a game where a child plays as a caregiver for animals teaches them to understand and respond to the needs and feelings of others.

2. **Emotional Literacy**: By engaging in role-playing, children learn to identify and articulate emotions, not only in themselves but also in the characters they embody. This enhances their emotional literacy, a key component of empathy.

3. **Social Situational Awareness**: RPGs can also enhance children's awareness of social situations and the different dynamics involved. Understanding the context and emotions of characters in various social settings can help children navigate similar situations in real life.

Cooperative Games for Teamwork Skills

Cooperative games are designed for players to work together towards a common goal, teaching essential lessons in teamwork and cooperation.

1. **Working Together**: Games that require children to collaborate teach them the value of working together. For instance, a puzzle game where each child controls a character that has a unique ability needed to solve the puzzle can teach the importance of teamwork.

2. **Sharing and Turn-Taking**: Cooperative games also foster skills like sharing and turn-taking. A game where children must share resources or take turns making decisions can help them understand the importance of fairness and patience.

3. **Problem-Solving as a Team**: These games often present challenges that cannot be solved by a single player, promoting collective problem-solving. Learning to listen to others' ideas and combine efforts to achieve a goal is a valuable skill for social interactions.

Conflict Resolution in Game Scenarios

Digital games can also be effective tools for teaching conflict resolution skills.

1. **Resolving Disputes in Game Play**: Games that include scenarios involving disputes between characters can teach children how to resolve conflicts. For instance, a game where players must help characters resolve a misunderstanding can teach children about listening, empathy, and finding peaceful solutions.

2. **Understanding Consequences of Actions**: Some games show the consequences of a player's actions on other characters, teaching children to consider the impact of their behavior. This can be an effective way to teach about cause and effect in social interactions.

3. **Negotiation and Compromise**: Games that involve negotiating with other characters or finding a middle ground can help develop skills in negotiation and compromise. Learning to find solutions that are acceptable to all parties is an essential aspect of resolving conflicts.

In conclusion, digital games offer diverse and effective ways to teach empathy, co-operation, and conflict resolution to preschoolers. Through role-playing, cooperative gameplay, and conflict resolution scenarios, children can learn and practice these essential social skills in a fun and engaging environment. These experiences not only enhance their immediate social interactions but also lay a foundation for their future personal and professional relationships.

23

Promoting Self-Regulation and Emotional Expression with Digital Games

Digital games can be powerful tools in aiding the development of self-regulation and emotional expression among preschoolers. By engaging in specifically designed games, children can learn to recognize, understand, and express their emotions more effectively, while also developing crucial self-regulation skills.

Games for Emotional Awareness

1. **Identifying and Labeling Emotions**: Games that focus on identifying and labeling emotions can be particularly effective in developing emotional awareness. For example, a game where children help a character navigate through different scenarios and choose how the character might feel in those situations can teach them to recognize various emotions. An example could be a game where a character faces various day-to-day challenges, and children have to select the emotion that the character is likely feeling, such as happiness, sadness, anger, or fear.

2. **Expressing Emotions**: Games that encourage children to express their own emotions can also be beneficial. For instance, digital drawing or storytelling apps where children create stories or artwork based on how they feel can provide a safe and creative outlet for emotional expression.

3. **Emotion-Themed Games**: Games specifically themed around emotions, such as those that involve recognizing facial expressions or body language associated with different feelings, can enhance children's ability to interpret and understand emotions in themselves and others.

Self-Regulation Through Game Challenges
   1. **Overcoming In-Game Obstacles**: Games that present challenges or obstacles require children to exercise self-regulation skills. For instance, a puzzle game that gradually increases in difficulty challenges children to remain focused and persistent, even when the task becomes challenging.

   2. **Managing Frustration**: Games can also teach children how to cope with frustration. In a game where a child must try multiple times to achieve a goal, they learn the importance of patience and perseverance. The game could provide encouragement and hints, helping children to manage frustration and try different strategies.

   3. **Rewarding Patience and Strategy**: Many games include mechanisms that reward patience and strategic thinking. For example, a game where players must wait for the right moment to make a move or collect items can teach children the value of waiting and planning.

   4. **Reflection and Adaptation**: Games that encourage reflection after a challenge, asking children how they felt and what they could do differently next time, can enhance self-regulation. This reflection helps children understand that they can control their reactions and adapt their strategies in challenging situations.

In summary, digital games can significantly contribute to the development of emotional awareness and self-regulation skills in preschoolers. Games that focus on identifying and expressing emotions help children become more aware of their feelings and those of others. Simultaneously, games that pose challenges and require perseverance and patience can teach valuable self-regulation skills. By incorporating these types of games into early childhood education, teachers and parents can provide children with fun and engaging ways to develop these critical emotional and cognitive skills.

24

STRATEGIES FOR FOSTERING SOCIAL INTERACTIONS DURING GAME-BASED LEARNING

Promoting social interactions in preschoolers through game-based learning can be a rewarding approach. It not only enhances their digital game experience but also fosters important social skills. Here are strategies to achieve this:

Encouraging Multiplayer Interactions

1. **Selecting Cooperative Multiplayer Games**: Choose games that require children to work together to achieve common goals. For example, games like "Animal Jam" allow children to explore virtual worlds and solve problems together, promoting teamwork and communication.

2. **Turn-Taking Games**: Games that involve turn-taking can teach patience and fairness. A simple game where children take turns controlling the game or making decisions can be effective.

3. **Problem-Solving as a Team**: Select games that pose challenges or puzzles that are best solved through collaboration. This approach encourages children to discuss, negotiate, and collectively strategize, building their teamwork and problem-solving skills.

4. **In-Game Communication**: Encourage games that have built-in communication features like chat (with appropriate safeguards) or in-game gestures. This helps children learn how to communicate and express themselves in a group setting.

Blending Digital and Real-World Socialization

1. **Post-Game Group Discussions**: After a digital game session, organize a group discussion where children can talk about their experience, what they learned, and how they felt. This helps in transferring the skills learned in the game to real-life scenarios.

2. **Collaborative Projects Based on Game Themes**: Engage children in collaborative projects or activities based on the themes or content of the digital games they've played. For instance, after playing a game about building a city, children could work together to create a model city using craft materials.

3. **Role-Play Activities**: Encourage role-play activities where children enact scenarios or characters from the games. This can help in deepening their understanding of the game's content and themes, while also fostering imagination and empathy.

Role of Educators in Facilitating Social Learning

1. **Guiding Group Interactions**: Educators play a vital role in guiding children's interactions during multiplayer game sessions. They can help in setting rules, moderating discussions, and ensuring that all children are actively involved.

2. **Using Games as Teachable Moments**: Digital game experiences can be used as teachable moments. Educators can highlight and discuss the importance of cooperation, kindness, and respect for others that emerge during gameplay.

3. **Encouraging Reflective Thinking**: Post-game, teachers can encourage children to reflect on their behavior and interactions during the game. This reflection can include questions about how they worked as a team, how they resolved conflicts, and what they would do differently next time.

4. **Incorporating Social Skills Objectives**: When planning game-based activities, educators can explicitly incorporate objectives related to social skills development, such as communication skills, emotional regulation, and empathy.

In conclusion, fostering social interactions during game-based learning involves a combination of carefully selecting appropriate games, blending digital experiences with real-world socialization, and the active role of educators in guiding and enhancing these interactions. By implementing these strategies, educators can create a rich, interactive, and socially engaging learning environment that extends beyond the digital realm.

Enhancing Cognitive Skills with Interactive Digital Games

As we venture into the digital age, the role of interactive digital games in enhancing cognitive skills in preschool education becomes increasingly significant. This introduction explores the multifaceted ways in which digital games can be utilized to bolster cognitive development in young children, setting a strong foundation for future learning and problem-solving abilities.

The early years are crucial for cognitive skills development, with the preschool period being particularly pivotal. During this time, children develop key cognitive skills such as memory, attention, reasoning, and problem-solving abilities. Understanding the natural progression of these skills and their impact on a child's overall development is essential for educators and parents alike. This section will emphasize the importance of nurturing these skills from a young age and how they form the bedrock of a child's learning journey.

Digital games in preschool education offer a unique avenue for enhancing these cognitive skills. By making learning more engaging and interactive, digital games have the potential to significantly improve the acquisition of cognitive abilities. This section will delve into how technology can be harnessed to support and enhance cognitive development in young learners, backed by insights from research on the cognitive benefits of digital gaming in early childhood education.

Specifically, the role of digital games in boosting memory, enhancing attention, and fostering problem-solving skills will be explored. This includes games that involve pattern recognition, sequencing, and recall activities for memory enhancement, as well as games that require sustained concentration and help develop selective attention skills. Additionally, the effectiveness of digital games in enhancing problem-solving abilities will be discussed, focusing on games that present logical puzzles and challenges.

Beyond these skills, digital games also play a crucial role in promoting critical thinking and creativity. This section will highlight how digital games can be used to develop critical thinking skills, encouraging children to question, hypothesize, and make informed decisions. Furthermore, the role of games in fostering creativity and imagination will be explored, including games that allow for open-ended play, exploration, and creative expression.

Integrating cognitive skill development into game-based learning requires strategic planning. This includes effectively incorporating cognitive skill-developing games into the preschool curriculum, balancing digital game-based learning with traditional learning methods, and tailoring game experiences to meet the diverse needs and skill levels of individual children. This section will provide practical strategies for educators to select appropriate games and incorporate them into daily learning activities, ensuring a holistic learning experience.

Finally, the critical role of educators and parents in guiding and supporting children's learning through digital games will be emphasized. This includes monitoring progress, providing feedback, and encouraging reflection on the learning experiences. By doing so, educators and parents can ensure that digital games are not only a source of entertainment but also a valuable tool for cognitive development in preschoolers.

In conclusion, this introduction underscores the immense potential of interactive digital games in enhancing cognitive skills in preschool education. By thoughtfully incorporating these digital tools into the learning process, educators and parents can create enriching, engaging, and effective learning experiences that lay a solid foundation for the cognitive development of young learners.

25

Cognitive Skills Development in Early Childhood

Cognitive skills development in early childhood shapes the foundation for lifelong learning, equipping young minds with the tools for understanding, problem-solving, and navigating the world around them.

Importance of Early Cognitive Development

The early years of a child's life are critical for cognitive development, which lays the foundation for future learning and intellectual growth. During this time, children undergo rapid brain development, which significantly impacts their ability to think, understand, process information, and solve problems.

1. **Building Blocks for Future Learning**: Early cognitive development is akin to building the foundation of a house; it sets the stage for all future learning. Skills developed during this period, such as language understanding, basic numeracy, and problem-solving, are crucial for academic success and everyday functioning.

2. **Impact on School Readiness**: The cognitive skills children develop in preschool play a significant role in preparing them for the structured learning environment of school. These early skills are predictive of later academic performance and are vital for a smooth transition to more formal schooling.

Key Cognitive Skills in Early Childhood

1. **Memory**: Memory development in preschoolers is essential for learning. Children begin to remember and recall information more effectively, which is crucial for all areas of learning, including language and math. For instance, being able to remember the alphabet is a foundational step in learning to read.

1. **Attention**: The ability to focus and maintain attention evolves significantly during the preschool years. Developing good attention skills is crucial for children to learn effectively. It enables them to concentrate on tasks, follow instructions, and complete learning activities.

2. **Reasoning**: Early childhood is a time when reasoning skills start to emerge. Children begin to understand cause and effect, make predictions based on past experiences, and solve simple problems. These reasoning skills are the building blocks for more complex thinking and decision-making abilities.

3. **Problem-Solving**: Problem-solving abilities develop as children learn to navigate challenges and obstacles in their environment. This skill is essential for academic tasks and everyday life. For example, figuring out how to construct a tower with blocks or solving a simple puzzle requires problem-solving skills.

4. **Language Development**: Cognitive development is closely tied to language skills. As children's brains develop, so does their ability to understand and use language. This includes expanding their vocabulary, understanding complex sentences, and beginning to grasp basic grammar rules.

5. **Executive Functioning**: This includes skills such as self-control, flexibility, and working memory. Children start to develop the ability to control their impulses, switch between tasks, and hold information in their mind while working on a task.

The development of these cognitive skills is a complex process that unfolds over time and is influenced by a child's environment, experiences, and the activities they engage in. Early childhood educators play a crucial role in supporting this development through carefully designed activities and learning experiences, including the use of digital games that are specifically tailored to enhance these cognitive skills.

In summary, understanding the significance of cognitive skills development in early childhood and the key cognitive abilities that emerge during this stage is essential for designing effective educational interventions and activities. This foundation is critical for children's overall development and future academic and personal success.

26

COGNITIVE BENEFITS OF USING DIGITAL GAMES IN PRESCHOOL EDUCATION

The integration of digital games in preschool education offers a unique blend of fun and learning, unlocking cognitive benefits that range from enhanced problem-solving abilities to improved memory and attention in young children.

Enhancing Learning Through Technology

1. **Engagement and Interactivity**: Digital games captivate children's attention through interactive and engaging content. This interactivity not only makes learning enjoyable but also enhances cognitive engagement. For instance, a game that uses animated characters and interactive puzzles to teach counting or letter recognition can significantly increase a child's interest and participation in learning these concepts.

2. **Multisensory Stimulation**: Digital games often involve multiple senses, including sight, sound, and touch. This multisensory approach can enhance cognitive processing and memory formation. For example, a game that combines visual elements, sound effects, and touch-based interactions for learning shapes can create a more memorable learning experience than traditional methods.

3. **Personalized Learning Paths**: Many digital games offer personalized learning experiences, adapting to a child's skill level. This personalization ensures that the game remains challenging but achievable, providing an optimal learning experience. For example, an adaptive math game can adjust the difficulty of problems based on the child's responses, ensuring that they are continuously challenged.

4. **Immediate Feedback and Reinforcement**: Digital games provide immediate feedback, which is crucial for learning. This instant response to a child's actions reinforces learning and helps them understand concepts more quickly. For instance, a game that immediately congratulates a child for correctly solving a math problem reinforces their understanding and boosts their confidence.

Research Insights

1. **Development of Specific Cognitive Skills**: Research has shown that certain digital games can aid in the development of specific cognitive skills such as problem-solving, logical reasoning, and spatial awareness. For example, puzzle games that require children to manipulate shapes and fit them into a space can enhance spatial reasoning skills.

2. **Improvement in Attention and Focus**: Studies have indicated that interactive digital games can improve attention and concentration in young children. Games that require sustained focus to achieve goals can help children develop their ability to concentrate over longer periods.

3. **Memory Enhancement**: Certain games are found to be effective in enhancing memory skills. For instance, games that involve remembering sequences or patterns can improve short-term and working memory in preschoolers.

4. **Executive Function Development**: Research also suggests that digital games can support the development of executive functions, such as cognitive flexibility, task-switching, and planning. Games that require children to think ahead, switch between tasks, or adapt to new rules can help in honing these higher-order cognitive skills.

5. **Language and Literacy Skills**: Educational games focusing on language and literacy can significantly impact these areas of cognitive development. Games that involve word recognition, phonetic learning, and vocabulary building can enhance language skills and prepare children for reading.

In conclusion, the use of digital games in preschool education offers substantial cognitive benefits. These games can make learning more dynamic and engaging, cater to individual learning needs, and provide immediate feedback. The insights from research underscore the potential of digital games to enhance various cognitive processes, making them valuable tools in early childhood education. By carefully selecting and integrating appropriate digital games, educators can significantly enrich the cognitive development of their students.

27

ENHANCING MEMORY, ATTENTION, AND PROBLEM-SOLVING THROUGH GAMES

Games present a playful yet potent medium for enhancing memory, sharpening attention, and honing problem-solving skills, turning complex cognitive development into an engaging and interactive experience.

Memory-Boosting Games
1. **Pattern Recognition and Sequencing**: Games that involve pattern recognition and sequencing are excellent for enhancing memory skills. For instance, a game like "Memory Match" or "Simon Says," where children need to remember and replicate sequences of colors, shapes, or sounds, can significantly boost short-term and working memory.

2. **Recall Activities**: Games that require children to recall information after a brief interval can strengthen memory retention. For example, "Hide and Seek" games, where objects are briefly shown and then hidden, require children to remember and find these objects.

3. **Story-Based Memory Games**: Digital story-based games where children need to remember and recount details of the story can enhance memory recall. These games can include interactive elements where children choose what happens next in the story based on what they remember from earlier parts.

Attention-Enhancing Games
1. **Sustained Concentration**: Games that require prolonged focus to complete tasks can improve attention spans. For example, puzzle games like "Tetris" or

"Bejeweled" where children need to concentrate for extended periods to achieve higher levels.

2. **Selective Attention Skills**: Games that require children to focus on specific elements amidst distractions can develop selective attention skills. For example, "I Spy" type games where children have to find specific items in a busy scene.

3. **Action Games for Quick Reflexes**: Fast-paced action games can also aid in developing attention skills. These games often require quick reflexes and sharp focus, helping children improve their ability to concentrate under dynamic conditions.

Problem-Solving Games

1. **Logical Reasoning Challenges**: Games that present logical challenges can enhance problem-solving skills. For example, games like "Rush Hour," where children have to navigate a car out of a traffic jam, require logical thinking and strategy planning.

2. **Critical Thinking Puzzles**: Puzzle games that require critical thinking, such as "Sudoku" or "Labyrinth" games, where children need to find paths or solve complex puzzles, can significantly improve problem-solving abilities.

3. **Adventure Games with Problem-Solving**: Adventure games that combine storytelling with problem-solving tasks can be particularly engaging. In these games, children need to solve puzzles to progress in the story, which helps in developing both their problem-solving skills and narrative understanding.

In conclusion, digital games can be a powerful tool in enhancing cognitive skills such as memory, attention, and problem-solving in preschoolers. These games provide fun and interactive ways to develop and strengthen these essential cognitive abilities, which are foundational for future academic success and everyday problem-solving. Carefully selected and appropriately used digital games can greatly contribute to the cognitive development of young children.

28

Promoting Critical Thinking and Creativity with Digital Games

Digital games stand at the forefront of modern learning, uniquely positioned to foster critical thinking and ignite creativity in a captivating, interactive digital landscape.

Critical Thinking

Digital games can be a powerful medium for nurturing critical thinking skills in young children. These skills are essential for children to analyze information, solve problems, and make reasoned decisions.

1. **Questioning and Exploration**: Games that encourage exploration and pose open-ended questions stimulate critical thinking. For instance, a game where children are presented with a scenario and must choose different outcomes based on their understanding can encourage them to think critically about the consequences of their actions.

2. **Hypothesizing and Testing**: Games that involve forming hypotheses and testing them are excellent for developing critical thinking. For example, a simple physics-based game where children need to predict the trajectory of an object and then test their hypothesis can be both fun and intellectually stimulating.

3. **Decision-Making Based on Information**: Strategy games, where children have to make decisions based on available information, can enhance their analytical skills. A game like "Zoombinis," where players solve puzzles using logical reasoning and pattern recognition, can encourage critical thinking.

4. **Problem-Solving in Complex Situations**: Games that present complex problems or puzzles can help develop advanced problem-solving skills. These games often require children to think several steps ahead and consider multiple variables, enhancing their ability to process information critically.

Creativity and Imagination

Digital games can also be a fertile ground for fostering creativity and imagination in preschoolers, allowing them to express themselves and explore various possibilities in a virtual environment.

1. **Open-Ended Play**: Games that offer open-ended play encourage creative thinking. For instance, sandbox games like "Toca Boca" where children can create their own worlds and stories provide a canvas for imaginative play and creativity.

2. **Artistic Expression**: Games that include drawing, music, and storytelling elements allow children to express their artistic abilities. For example, a game like "Artie's Magic Pencil," where children use drawing to solve problems and rebuild a virtual world, encourages creative thinking and artistic expression.

3. **Exploratory Games**: Games that encourage exploration, such as those set in large open worlds or with multiple paths and outcomes, can stimulate a child's imagination. These games allow children to explore different scenarios and create their own narratives within the game.

4. **Interactive Storytelling**: Storytelling games where children can choose different paths or create their own stories can greatly enhance creativity. These games often allow children to explore various narrative possibilities, encouraging them to use their imagination to create unique stories.

In summary, digital games can be effectively used to promote both critical thinking and creativity in young children. By engaging in games that challenge them to think critically and creatively, children can develop these essential skills in a fun and interactive way. These skills are not only crucial for academic success but also for overall intellectual and personal development.

29

STRATEGIES FOR INCORPORATING COGNITIVE SKILL DEVELOPMENT IN GAME-BASED LEARNING

Incorporating cognitive skill development into game-based learning involves strategic selection of games, balancing digital experiences with traditional methods, and tailoring activities to individual learner needs for a holistic educational approach.

Integrating Games into the Curriculum

1. **Strategic Selection of Games**: Choose games that align with specific educational goals of the curriculum. For example, select puzzle games for problem-solving skills, memory games for cognitive development, and story-based games for language and literacy skills.

2. **Integrating Games with Lesson Plans**: Incorporate digital games into lesson plans as a complementary tool. For instance, use a math game as part of a larger lesson on counting or addition, allowing children to apply what they've learned in an interactive format.

3. **Thematic Integration**: Align games with current classroom themes or topics. If the theme is 'Under the Sea', use games that incorporate sea creatures and underwater environments to teach various concepts.

4. **Scheduling Game Time**: Allocate specific times for game-based learning, ensuring it complements other learning activities rather than replacing them. This could be a dedicated 'game hour' where educational games are played to reinforce the day's learning.

Balancing Digital and Traditional Learning

1. **Combining Digital with Hands-On Activities**: After a digital game session, engage children in hands-on activities that relate to the game's content. For instance, if they played a digital game about planting seeds, follow it with a real-world activity of planting seeds in the classroom.

2. **Ensuring Varied Learning Experiences**: Provide a mix of digital and non-digital learning experiences. While digital games are effective for certain types of learning, traditional activities like storytelling, arts and crafts, and physical play are essential for a well-rounded education.

3. **Limiting Screen Time**: Be mindful of the screen time guidelines for young children. Balance digital game time with other educational activities that do not involve screens.

Tailoring Games to Individual Needs

1. **Customizable Game Settings**: Select games that offer customizable settings to cater to different learning abilities and preferences. This might include adjustable difficulty levels, the option to choose different activities within the game, and varying lengths of game time.

2. **Adaptive Learning Technology**: Use games equipped with adaptive learning technology that automatically adjusts the difficulty level based on the child's performance, ensuring a tailored learning experience.

3. **Observing Individual Responses**: Pay attention to how each child interacts with the game and adjust the game experience accordingly. If a child finds a game too challenging or too easy, find more suitable alternatives.

Role of Educators and Parents

1. **Active Involvement and Monitoring**: Educators and parents should actively involve themselves in the child's game-based learning. This includes playing games with the children, monitoring their progress, and discussing the games' content.

2. **Providing Constructive Feedback**: Offer feedback and encouragement. Discuss what the child learned from the game and ask questions that prompt

reflection on the game experience.

3. **Encouraging Real-World Application**: Help children make connections between what they learn in games and real-world scenarios. For example, if a child plays a game about shapes, point out similar shapes in the environment.

4. **Ensuring a Safe Gaming Environment**: Ensure that the gaming environment is safe and age-appropriate. This includes monitoring the content of the games and ensuring they are suitable for preschoolers.

In conclusion, effectively incorporating cognitive skill development in game-based learning requires a thoughtful approach that includes selecting appropriate games, balancing digital with traditional learning methods, tailoring games to individual needs, and active involvement from educators and parents. By employing these strategies, digital games can become a valuable part of a comprehensive and diverse preschool curriculum.

Promoting Language and Literacy with Digital Games

In the dynamic and interactive world of preschool education, digital games are emerging as powerful tools in promoting language and literacy development. This introduction provides an overview of how these innovative tools can be harnessed to enhance key language and literacy skills in young learners, setting the stage for their communication, academic success, and lifelong learning.

Language and literacy development play a foundational role in early childhood. These skills are crucial for effective communication and form the basis for academic learning and future educational success. The process of language acquisition in young children is multifaceted, involving the development of vocabulary, grammar, and the ability to understand and use language effectively. This introduction underscores the importance of nurturing these skills from an early age and lays the groundwork for discussing how digital games can facilitate this development.

Interactive digital games offer a unique and engaging approach to language learning. By incorporating multimedia elements such as sound, visuals, and text, these games make language learning more enjoyable and effective for young children. This section will explore the advantages of interactive digital games in language acquisition, focusing on how they can provide customizable learning experiences that adapt to each child's language level and pace.

Specifically, the role of digital games in vocabulary building will be discussed. Games that involve word recognition, categorization, and usage in context are particularly effective in expanding a child's vocabulary. The importance of contextual learning will be highlighted, emphasizing how digital games can simulate real-life scenarios for practical application of new words.

In addition to vocabulary development, digital games are instrumental in promoting phonological awareness and early reading skills. This section will describe how games can help develop phonological awareness, a critical skill for reading, including recognizing and manipulating sounds in spoken language. The discussion will also cover games that introduce basic reading skills such as letter recognition, sound-letter correspondence, and simple word reading.

Digital storytelling and writing activities are also vital components of language and literacy development. This introduction will explore how digital storytelling games can enhance narrative skills and understanding of story structure, as well as how digital games can introduce basic writing and composition skills, including forming letters and creating simple sentences.

Finally, the crucial role of educators and parents in this process will be discussed. This includes selecting appropriate games, guiding children through game-based learning activities, and integrating these games into a broader language and literacy curriculum. By actively participating in and overseeing children's interactions with digital games, educators and parents can ensure that these tools are used effectively to bolster language and literacy development.

In conclusion, this introduction sets the foundation for understanding how interactive digital games can be effectively utilized in preschool settings to enhance language and literacy skills. It highlights the potential of these digital tools in creating engaging, effective, and personalized learning experiences that can significantly contribute to the early development of vital communication and reading skills in young learners.

30

IMPORTANCE OF LANGUAGE AND LITERACY DEVELOPMENT IN PRESCHOOL

Language and literacy form the bedrock of early childhood education, serving as essential tools for communication, academic success, and cognitive growth.

Foundational Role of Language and Literacy

Language and literacy are crucial in early childhood development, serving as fundamental building blocks for a child's overall growth and future academic success.

1. **Basis for Communication**: Language skills acquired during preschool years form the basis for effective communication. The ability to express thoughts, feelings, and ideas clearly is essential not only for academic purposes but also for everyday interactions.

2. **Academic Success**: Proficiency in language and literacy is closely linked to academic achievement. Children who develop strong reading and writing skills early on are more likely to perform better in school. Literacy skills enable children to engage with educational content more effectively, understand instructions, and participate actively in classroom activities.

3. **Cognitive Development**: Language development is intertwined with cognitive development. As children learn new words and how to structure sentences, their thinking and understanding of the world also expand. This linguistic growth contributes to their problem-solving skills, creativity, and critical thinking abilities.

1. **Lifelong Learning**: Early literacy experiences lay a foundation for lifelong learning. Children who develop a love for reading and writing from a young age are likely to continue being engaged learners throughout their lives.

Early Language Acquisition

The process of language acquisition in young children involves several stages, each critical to developing a full understanding and use of language.

1. **Vocabulary Development**: Young children rapidly expand their vocabulary as they are exposed to new words in their environment. This vocabulary growth enhances their ability to communicate more effectively and understand the world around them. Games that introduce new words in a fun and interactive way, such as those where children match pictures with words, can be particularly effective.

2. **Learning Grammar**: Preschoolers begin to grasp basic grammatical structures, enabling them to form more complex sentences. Digital games that involve constructing sentences or using words in context can support this aspect of language development.

3. **Understanding and Using Language**: As children's vocabulary and grammar skills develop, so does their ability to understand and effectively use language. Interactive storytelling games, where children choose what happens next in the story, can encourage them to use language for decision-making and predicting outcomes.

4. **Listening Skills**: Language acquisition also involves the development of listening skills. Games that require children to follow verbal instructions or listen to stories and answer questions about them can enhance their listening comprehension.

In conclusion, the development of language and literacy skills in preschool is critical for a child's communication abilities, academic success, cognitive development, and lifelong learning. The use of digital games in early education can support this development by providing interactive, engaging, and educational experiences that enhance language acquisition and literacy skills.

31

HOW DIGITAL GAMES CAN FACILITATE LANGUAGE ACQUISITION AND LITERACY SKILLS

Digital games offer a dynamic and interactive platform for facilitating language acquisition and literacy skills, blending engaging content with educational strategies to enhance children's linguistic abilities.

Interactive Language Learning

1. **Engagement through Multimedia Elements**: Digital games leverage a combination of sound, visuals, and interactive text to create a rich, engaging language learning environment. For example, games that use colorful animations and characters to introduce new words can make the learning experience more appealing and memorable for children. An interactive game like "Endless Alphabet" uses animations and sounds to teach letter recognition and vocabulary, making the experience both educational and entertaining.

2. **Enhancing Pronunciation and Listening Skills**: Games with spoken instructions or narratives can help children improve their pronunciation and listening skills. For example, a story-based game with narrated content enables children to hear and practice proper pronunciation, improving their language comprehension and spoken skills.

3. **Interactive Storytelling**: Digital games that include storytelling elements allow children to engage with narratives actively. This not only enhances their understanding of the language but also develops their ability to follow and comprehend stories. A game where children choose different outcomes in a story can also encourage them to think critically about the narrative and its

language.

4. **Visual and Auditory Reinforcement**: The combination of visual cues with auditory feedback in games reinforces language learning. When children associate words with images and sounds, it strengthens their ability to recall and use these words effectively.

Customizable Learning Experiences

1. **Adapting to Individual Learning Paces**: Many digital language learning games are designed to adapt to the individual learning pace of each child. This means that the game's difficulty level adjusts based on the child's responses, providing a personalized learning experience. For instance, a game might offer simpler vocabulary initially and gradually introduce more complex words as the child's understanding improves.

2. **Choice of Language Activities**: Offering a variety of language activities within a game caters to different learning styles and preferences. For example, a game might include options for word matching, sentence construction, and story creation, allowing children to engage with language learning in multiple ways.

3. **Progress Tracking and Feedback**: Digital games often include progress tracking and provide feedback to children and educators. This feature enables monitoring of language development, allowing educators and parents to understand the child's progress and areas where additional support might be needed.

4. **Catering to Diverse Linguistic Backgrounds**: Digital games can be particularly beneficial for children from diverse linguistic backgrounds. Games available in multiple languages or those that focus on basic English language skills can help non-native speakers develop their language proficiency in an engaging and stress-free environment.

In summary, digital games present a unique opportunity to facilitate language acquisition and literacy skills in preschoolers. Through interactive learning experiences and customizable activities, these games can make language learning more engaging, effective, and tailored to the individual needs of each child. By integrating sound, visuals, and interactivity, digital games offer a dynamic approach to language education that can significantly enhance a child's linguistic abilities.

32

SUPPORTING VOCABULARY DEVELOPMENT THROUGH GAME-BASED LEARNING

Game-based learning supports vocabulary development by offering interactive and enjoyable ways for children to encounter, understand, and use new words, enriching their language skills through play.

Vocabulary Building Games

1. **Word Recognition Games**: Digital games that focus on word recognition are fundamental for building vocabulary in young children. For example, games like "Sight Words" involve children identifying and selecting words from a list or within a story. These games often include a variety of levels, starting with simple words and progressing to more complex vocabulary.

2. **Categorization Games**: Games that involve sorting and categorizing words can enhance a child's understanding of language and its use. For instance, a game where children categorize items by their attributes, such as color, shape, or size, can expand their descriptive vocabulary. An example is "Montessori Crosswords," which helps children learn words based on sound categories.

3. **Usage in Context**: Games that teach vocabulary through context help children understand how words are used in sentences and real-life situations. A game like "My Word Coach" presents words within the context of sentences, enhancing comprehension and usage skills.

4. **Interactive Spelling Games**: Games that combine spelling activities with vocabulary learning can be particularly effective. For instance, "Spelling City"

offers a range of interactive spelling games that also reinforce word meanings, making it an excellent tool for comprehensive vocabulary development.

Contextual Learning

1. **Simulating Real-Life Scenarios**: Digital games that simulate real-life scenarios can provide a context for new vocabulary. For instance, a game set in a grocery store could introduce words related to food, money, and quantities, teaching children vocabulary relevant to everyday situations.

2. **Story-Based Learning**: Games that use narratives and storytelling can introduce new words within the context of a story, making it easier for children to understand and remember them. For example, a story-based game where children follow characters on an adventure can introduce thematic vocabulary related to the story's setting and plot.

3. **Role-Playing Games**: RPGs allow children to step into different roles and scenarios, encountering new words in varied contexts. A game where children play as chefs, doctors, or astronauts, for example, exposes them to specific vocabulary related to these professions.

4. **Learning Through Exploration**: Exploration-based games encourage children to discover new words interactively. A game where children explore different environments, such as a jungle or ocean, can introduce them to the relevant vocabulary in an engaging and memorable way.

5. **Enhancing Comprehension**: Contextual learning in games not only aids in vocabulary acquisition but also enhances overall comprehension. By learning words in context, children are more likely to understand their meanings and use them correctly in communication.

In summary, supporting vocabulary development through game-based learning involves using digital games that focus on word recognition, categorization, usage in context, and real-life scenarios. These games provide an interactive and engaging platform for children to expand their vocabulary and understand the application of new words in various contexts. By integrating vocabulary learning into fun and relatable scenarios, digital games can significantly enhance a child's language skills and overall linguistic development.

33

Promoting Phonological Awareness and Early Reading Skills with Games

Games play a pivotal role in promoting phonological awareness and early reading skills, transforming the learning of sounds, letters, and words into an enjoyable and engaging experience for young learners.

Phonics and Phonemic Awareness Games
1. **Sound Recognition and Manipulation**: Games that focus on phonics and phonemic awareness can significantly aid in developing reading skills. These games teach children to recognize and manipulate individual sounds in spoken words, a foundational skill for reading. For example, a game like "Phonics Ninja" allows children to 'slice' through letters and sounds, reinforcing their ability to identify different phonemes.

2. **Rhyming and Alliteration Games**: Games that involve rhyming and alliteration can be fun ways to enhance phonological awareness. For instance, a game where children match rhyming words or create silly alliterative sentences can make learning sounds enjoyable and engaging.

3. **Blending and Segmenting Sounds**: Digital games that focus on blending sounds to form words and segmenting words into individual sounds can strengthen phonemic awareness. An app like "Reading Eggs" includes activities where children blend sounds to create words and break words down into their constituent sounds.

Early Reading Games

1. **Letter Recognition Games**: Games that teach letter recognition lay the groundwork for reading. These games often involve matching letters with objects that start with that letter, helping children associate letters with sounds. A game like "ABC Mouse" offers a variety of activities that focus on recognizing and naming letters.

2. **Sound-Letter Correspondence**: Games that teach the correspondence between sounds and letters are crucial for developing reading skills. For example, a game where children hear a sound and then have to choose the corresponding letter or vice versa helps in establishing this fundamental connection.

3. **Simple Word Reading**: Games that encourage the reading of simple words can be very beneficial for early readers. These might include games where children have to form words from a given set of letters or read and match simple words with pictures. A game like "Endless Reader" introduces children to word formation and reading in a playful and interactive way.

4. **Sequential Reading Games**: Games that gradually increase in complexity, starting with letter recognition, moving to sound-letter correspondence, and then to word reading, can provide a sequential approach to reading. This scaffolding ensures that children build on their skills progressively.

5. **Interactive eBooks**: Digital interactive books can also be a form of game-based learning. These eBooks often include clickable words or phrases, where children can hear the pronunciation and see animations that explain the word's meaning, making the reading experience more engaging and informative.

In summary, promoting phonological awareness and early reading skills through games involves using digital platforms that focus on phonics, sound manipulation, letter recognition, and simple word reading. These games provide an interactive and enjoyable way for children to develop the foundational skills necessary for reading. By integrating these elements into game-based learning, educators and parents can significantly enhance a child's early reading abilities and overall language development.

34

INTEGRATING DIGITAL STORYTELLING AND WRITING ACTIVITIES IN GAME-BASED LEARNING

Integrating digital storytelling and writing activities in game-based learning empowers children to creatively express themselves and enhance their language skills in an immersive, interactive environment.

Digital Storytelling

1. **Enhancing Narrative Skills**: Digital storytelling games can significantly enhance children's narrative skills. These games often allow children to create their own stories or influence the direction of an existing story. For example, a game like "Toontastic 3D" enables children to create their own animated stories, choosing characters, settings, and plot developments, which helps them understand story structure and boosts their creativity.

2. **Understanding Story Structure**: Games that involve constructing stories can teach children about the beginning, middle, and end of stories, as well as other elements like character development and plot twists. This not only enhances their understanding of how stories are built but also encourages them to think critically about storytelling elements.

3. **Interactive Elements**: Digital storytelling often includes interactive elements that make stories more engaging. Children might choose different paths for a character, solve puzzles to move the story forward, or make decisions that affect the story's outcome. This interactivity can make the learning process more dynamic and enjoyable.

Writing and Composition
1. **Forming Letters**: Digital games can be used to introduce young children to letter formation. Games that involve tracing letters on a touchscreen or using a mouse to follow letter shapes can develop fine motor skills and familiarize children with the alphabet. For example, "Letter School" offers engaging ways to practice letter tracing.

2. **Creating Simple Sentences**: Once children are familiar with letters, games can help them progress to forming simple words and sentences. Games that involve word matching, sentence completion, or simple storytelling can encourage children to start constructing sentences, enhancing their writing skills.

3. **Expressing Ideas in Written Form**: Advanced games can encourage children to express their ideas through writing. This might involve games where children write short descriptions for characters or scenes, or even contribute to a collaborative story with other players.

Role of Educators and Parents
1. **Selecting Appropriate Games**: Educators and parents play a crucial role in selecting games that are suitable for their children's age and literacy level. They should look for games that align with their educational goals and are engaging and age-appropriate.

2. **Guiding Game-Based Learning**: Active involvement in guiding children through game-based learning activities is important. This includes helping them understand the instructions, encouraging them to express their ideas, and discussing the content of the games to reinforce learning.

3. **Integrating Games into Learning**: Educators and parents should integrate digital games into a broader language and literacy curriculum. This integration can include pre- and post-game activities that complement the skills learned in the game, such as drawing pictures of a story from a game or writing a physical letter after practicing letter formation in a game.

4. **Monitoring and Feedback**: Monitoring children's progress and providing feedback is essential. This helps in understanding how effectively the games are contributing to the child's language and literacy development and allows for

adjustments in the selection and use of games.

In conclusion, integrating digital storytelling and writing activities in game-based learning can significantly enhance language and literacy skills in preschoolers. By allowing children to interact with and create stories, and by introducing basic writing and composition skills, digital games provide a dynamic and interactive platform for literacy development. The role of educators and parents in guiding and supporting this process is pivotal to maximize the benefits of digital game-based learning in developing language and literacy skills.

Encouraging Physical Activity and Motor Skills through Digital Games

In the vibrant and ever-evolving world of preschool education, the incorporation of digital games presents a novel opportunity to promote physical activity and motor skill development in young children. This introduction explores how digital games can be ingeniously utilized to encourage movement, coordination, and overall physical development, aligning with the essential needs of early childhood growth.

Physical activity and motor skills development play a crucial role in the early stages of a child's life. These skills are fundamental to a child's overall health and development, aiding in building strength, coordination, and balance. This introduction emphasizes the importance of these skills and discusses the integral role of fine and gross motor skills in preschoolers' learning and daily activities, including the development of abilities such as balance, coordination, and manual dexterity.

One innovative approach to enhancing physical development in young children is through active gaming. Digital games can be designed to encourage physical movement, with examples ranging from dance games to those simulating sports activities. This section will explore how such games can make physical activity fun and engaging, thereby promoting a more active lifestyle in preschoolers.

Augmented Reality (AR) games are another exciting avenue for promoting physical activity. By blending virtual elements with the real world, AR games encourage children to move, explore, and interact with their environment in active ways. This introduction will discuss the potential of AR games in fostering an enjoyable and physically engaging play experience.

Integrating active play and exercise into game-based learning is a key strategy for fostering physical development. This includes combining digital and physical play, such as transitioning from a digital gardening game to actual gardening activities, and gamifying exercise to make physical activity more appealing to children. This section will offer strategies for integrating physical activities into digital gaming sessions and discuss how digital tools can be used to track movement and set physical challenges.

The use of motion-controlled games to enhance motor skill development is another focus area. This section will describe how these games can be tailored to improve fine motor skills, such as requiring precise hand movements or dexterity, and develop gross motor skills, like jumping, running, or balancing, through games that involve mimicking movements or completing physical challenges.

Balancing screen time with physical activity is essential in the context of preschool education. This introduction will provide guidance on creating a balanced routine that includes both screen time and active play. It will emphasize the role of educators and parents in monitoring screen time and fostering an environment that encourages physical activity. Additionally, the importance of outdoor play will be highlighted, along with strategies for using digital games to complement rather than replace outdoor activities.

In conclusion, this introduction sets the stage for a comprehensive exploration of how digital games can be effectively used in preschool settings to enhance physical activity and motor skills development. By thoughtfully integrating these innovative tools into the learning process, educators and parents can create enriching, engaging, and healthy learning experiences that foster physical development and lay the foundation for a lifetime of health and well-being.

35

Importance of Physical Activity and Motor Skills Development in Preschool

Physical activity and motor skills development are crucial in preschool, laying the foundation for children's overall health, coordination, and integration of cognitive and social skills.

Essential Role of Physical Development

Physical development in early childhood is a critical aspect of overall health and wellbeing. It plays a key role not only in the physical growth of young children but also in their cognitive and emotional development.

1. **Building a Healthy Foundation**: Regular physical activity is essential for the healthy growth of bones, muscles, and joints. It also helps in developing cardiovascular health and maintaining a healthy weight. Active play and physical games are crucial for building this foundation in preschoolers.

2. **Enhancing Cognitive Development**: Physical activity is closely linked to cognitive development. Activities that involve coordination, movement, and exploration contribute to the development of neural pathways. This brain development is important for cognitive functions like attention, memory, and problem-solving.

3. **Emotional Wellbeing**: Engaging in physical activity can significantly impact emotional wellbeing. Active play promotes the release of endorphins, which are natural mood lifters. It also provides a healthy outlet for stress and anxiety, helping children manage their emotions more effectively.

Motor Skills in Early Learning

Motor skills development is a vital part of early childhood education, as it directly impacts children's ability to engage with their environment and learn new skills.

1. **Fine Motor Skills**: Fine motor skills involve the use of small muscles in the hands and fingers. These skills are crucial for tasks like writing, drawing, cutting with scissors, and manipulating small objects. Activities such as playing with building blocks, drawing shapes, or threading beads help in developing these skills.

2. **Gross Motor Skills**: Gross motor skills utilize larger muscle groups for activities like running, jumping, and climbing. These skills are important for overall physical health and coordination. Activities like playing catch, hopping on one foot, or navigating obstacle courses can enhance gross motor skills.

3. **Balance and Coordination**: Activities that require balance and coordination are important for motor skill development. This includes activities like balancing on a beam, riding a tricycle, or participating in dance and movement games.

4. **Integration with Cognitive and Social Learning**: Motor skills development is often integrated with cognitive and social learning. For example, a game that involves a physical activity requiring teamwork can help develop motor skills while also teaching important social skills like cooperation and communication.

In conclusion, the development of physical activity and motor skills in preschool is crucial for children's overall health, cognitive development, and emotional wellbeing. Engaging children in a variety of physical activities and games can significantly contribute to their motor skills development, preparing them for more complex learning and interactions in the future.

36

HOW DIGITAL GAMES CAN PROMOTE PHYSICAL MOVEMENT AND COORDINATION

Digital games can promote physical movement and coordination in children by incorporating engaging activities that blend screen-based interaction with dynamic physical play, enhancing both motor skills and overall physical health.

Active Gaming

Active gaming, also known as "exergaming," has revolutionized the way children interact with digital games by integrating physical activity into the gaming experience.

1. **Dance and Rhythm Games**: Dance and rhythm games are prime examples of active gaming. Games like "Just Dance Kids" involve children following on-screen dance moves, encouraging them to move rhythmically to the music. These games not only promote physical activity but also help in developing coordination and rhythm.

2. **Sports Simulation Games**: Sports simulation games allow children to engage in virtual sports activities. For example, games that simulate tennis, soccer, or basketball require children to perform physical movements corresponding to those sports, providing a fun and interactive way to engage in physical activity.

3. **Fitness and Yoga Games**: Some digital games focus on fitness routines and yoga for children. These games guide children through various exercises and yoga poses, promoting flexibility, balance, and overall physical fitness.

4. **Interactive Adventure Games**: Games that require players to complete physical challenges as part of an adventure or quest can be highly engaging. For

instance, a game that involves jumping, ducking, or running in place to navigate through virtual worlds can be both entertaining and physically stimulating.

Augmented Reality (AR) Games

Augmented Reality (AR) games blend the digital and physical worlds, creating unique opportunities for movement and exploration.

1. **Exploration and Discovery**: AR games like "Pokémon GO" encourage children to explore their real-world environment while interacting with virtual elements. These games often require walking, running, or navigating to specific locations, thereby promoting physical activity.

2. **Real-World Interaction**: AR games can transform everyday spaces into interactive gaming environments. For instance, a game that turns a playground or backyard into a virtual treasure hunt encourages children to move around, search for items, and complete physical challenges.

3. **Educational AR Games**: There are AR games designed with educational purposes in mind, such as exploring natural habitats or historical sites. These games can motivate children to walk and explore while learning about various subjects.

4. **Enhancing Motor Skills with AR**: AR games can also be tailored to target specific motor skills. For example, a game that requires children to catch virtual objects or interact with elements at different heights and positions can help improve hand-eye coordination and spatial awareness.

In conclusion, digital games, especially active and AR games, offer innovative ways to promote physical movement and coordination in children. By integrating physical activity into the gaming experience, these games provide a fun and interactive platform for children to enhance their physical abilities, including coordination, balance, and overall fitness. The use of technology in this way represents a positive step towards addressing concerns about sedentary behavior associated with traditional digital gaming.

37

Integrating Active Play and Exercise in Game-Based Learning

Integrating active play and exercise in game-based learning involves creating a balanced blend of digital engagement and physical activities, fostering motor skill development alongside cognitive growth in an enjoyable, interactive manner.

Combining Digital and Physical Play

1. **Seamless Transitions from Virtual to Real**: Create learning experiences that begin with a digital game and then transition into a related real-world activity. For example, a game that involves virtual gardening or farm management can be followed by actual gardening activities, where children plant seeds or tend to a garden. This approach reinforces the concepts learned in the game and encourages children to apply them in a tangible way.

2. **Interactive Story-Based Activities**: Use digital storytelling games that require children to complete certain physical tasks to progress the story. For instance, a game could involve a story where characters need to cross a river, followed by a real-life activity where children hop across designated "stepping stones" in the classroom.

3. **Thematic Physical Challenges**: Design physical challenges based on the themes of digital games. If a game involves exploring space, for example, follow it up with a physical activity where children pretend to be astronauts doing exercises to prepare for space travel.

1. **Incorporating Role-Play**: Utilize role-playing elements from digital games in physical activities. If children play a game as characters with specific roles, they can then act out these roles in a physical setting, such as pretending to be explorers on a treasure hunt.

Gamifying Exercise

1. **Fitness Tracking and Reward Systems**: Use digital tools like fitness trackers to gamify physical exercise. Set challenges for children, like walking a certain number of steps or completing a set of exercises, and reward them with digital badges or points. This approach can make the exercise feel more like a game and less like a chore.

2. **Interactive Exercise Games**: Incorporate digital exercise games that use motion sensing technology. Games like "Zumba Kids" or "Wii Fit" encourage children to perform physical exercises through fun and interactive gameplay, blending fitness with digital entertainment.

3. **Augmented Reality (AR) Fitness Challenges**: Utilize AR technology to create immersive fitness experiences. For instance, an AR game could have children chasing after virtual creatures in their play area, encouraging them to run, jump, and move around.

4. **Creating Custom Exercise Routines**: Develop custom exercise routines that mimic game scenarios. If a game involves adventure or exploration, create an obstacle course or a series of physical challenges that mimic the adventures in the game.

In conclusion, integrating active play and exercise into game-based learning involves creative strategies that bridge the gap between the virtual and physical worlds. By combining digital gameplay with related physical activities and gamifying exercise through technology and imaginative scenarios, educators can make physical activity a fun and integral part of the learning experience. This approach not only enhances physical development but also reinforces the concepts learned through digital games, creating a comprehensive and engaging learning environment.

38

USING MOTION-CONTROLLED GAMES TO ENHANCE MOTOR SKILL DEVELOPMENT

U tilizing motion-controlled games in learning harnesses technology to enhance motor skill development, offering an innovative way for children to engage in physical activity while interacting with a digital environment.

Fine Motor Skills

Motion-controlled games, which require specific hand movements and dexterity, can significantly improve fine motor skills in young children.

1. **Precision-Based Games**: Games that require precise hand movements, like drawing shapes or tracing paths on a screen, can improve fine motor skills and hand-eye coordination. For instance, a game where children use a stylus or their fingers to trace letters or shapes helps develop control and precision in hand movements.

2. **Interactive Crafting Games**: Some games simulate crafting activities, such as building, sculpting, or painting, which require detailed hand movements. These games can help children practice the delicate control of their fingers and hands, enhancing their dexterity.

3. **Puzzle and Assembly Games**: Games that involve assembling parts or solving puzzles by manipulating small virtual pieces can be beneficial. These activities require children to use careful hand movements, improving their fine motor skills and spatial awareness.

Gross Motor Skills

Games that involve whole-body movement can be excellent for developing gross motor skills, which include larger movements involving arms, legs, feet, or the entire body.

1. **Movement Mimicry Games**: Games that require children to mimic movements can enhance gross motor skills. For instance, a game where children imitate animal movements—like hopping like a frog or stretching like a cat—encourages them to use different muscle groups.

2. **Sports and Action Games**: Motion-controlled sports games, where children engage in activities like virtual bowling, tennis, or soccer, require them to make broad physical movements. These games can improve overall body coordination, balance, and strength.

3. **Rhythm and Dance Games**: Dance games are particularly effective for gross motor skill development. They require children to move in time with music, often following complex sequences of movements. This not only improves their coordination and rhythm but also enhances their physical fitness.

4. **Adventure and Exploration Games**: Some games involve navigating through virtual environments, encouraging children to perform physical actions like jumping, turning, or balancing in place. These types of games can be exciting and engaging ways to develop gross motor skills.

5. **Fitness and Yoga Games**: Games that focus on fitness routines or yoga poses can also be beneficial. They can guide children through a series of physical exercises or yoga positions, promoting flexibility, balance, and muscle strength.

In conclusion, motion-controlled games offer a unique and engaging way to enhance both fine and gross motor skills in children. By incorporating precise hand movements, whole-body activities, and various physical challenges, these games provide an interactive platform for children to develop essential motor skills while having fun. The use of such technology in early education represents a valuable tool for physical development, complementing traditional forms of physical and motor skill training.

39

STRATEGIES FOR BALANCING SCREEN TIME WITH PHYSICAL ACTIVITY IN PRESCHOOL

Balancing screen time with physical activity in preschool involves setting clear guidelines for digital engagement, incorporating regular active play intervals, and integrating screen-based learning with dynamic physical exercises.

Creating a Balanced Routine
1. **Scheduled Screen Time**: Establish a schedule that clearly defines the times for screen-based activities and physical play. For example, limit digital game time to specific hours of the day and ensure it is followed by a period of physical activity. This could be structured as an hour of digital learning followed by outdoor play or a physical activity session.

2. **Active Breaks**: Incorporate short, active breaks between screen time sessions. For instance, after 20 minutes of playing a digital game, children can engage in a 10-minute physical activity like stretching, jumping jacks, or a quick game of tag.

3. **Combining Learning with Movement**: Use digital games that integrate learning with physical movement. Games that require children to stand, jump, or use hand-eye coordination can serve as both educational tools and sources of physical activity.

4. **Evening Unplugged Time**: Encourage an 'unplugged' period in the evening, focusing on non-screen activities like playing outside, physical indoor games, or family walks.

Educator and Parental Involvement
1. **Active Monitoring**: Educators and parents should actively monitor both the amount and content of screen time. This includes understanding the games children are playing and ensuring they offer some educational or physical value.

2. **Setting an Example**: Adults can set an example by participating in physical activities themselves. Joining children in active play or exercise routines can encourage them to be more physically active.

3. **Balancing Screen Time with Interactive Play**: Encourage parents and educators to balance digital game time with interactive play that promotes physical movement. This can include setting up relay races, obstacle courses, or dance sessions that are fun and engaging.

4. **Educational Workshops**: Schools and communities can offer workshops for parents and educators on the importance of balancing screen time with physical activity, providing them with practical strategies and ideas.

Encouraging Outdoor Play
1. **Linking Digital Themes with Outdoor Activities**: If children are playing a digital game with a specific theme, such as wildlife or sports, educators and parents can organize related outdoor activities. For instance, a digital game about wildlife can be complemented with a nature walk or outdoor scavenger hunt.

2. **Technology-Assisted Outdoor Exploration**: Use technology to enhance outdoor experiences. This might include using apps for identifying plants and animals during a nature walk or engaging in geocaching adventures.

3. **Setting 'No Screen' Zones and Times**: Establish specific zones, such as playgrounds and outdoor areas, as 'no screen' zones. Additionally, allocate certain times of the day, especially during good weather, exclusively for outdoor activities.

4. **Community-Based Activities**: Encourage participation in community sports teams, outdoor group activities, or local events. This not only promotes physical activity but also helps in developing social skills.

In summary, balancing screen time with physical activity in preschool requires a multi-faceted approach, including creating a structured routine, active involvement from educators and parents, and a strong emphasis on outdoor play. By integrating these strategies, children can enjoy the benefits of digital learning while also engaging in necessary physical activities for their overall development.

Engaging Parents and Caregivers in Game-Based Learning

In the realm of preschool education, the engagement of parents and caregivers in game-based learning is not just beneficial but essential. This introduction explores the pivotal role that parents and caregivers play in the early developmental stages of a child's education, particularly in the context of integrating digital games as educational tools.

The involvement of parents and caregivers in a child's early education is critical. Their role in influencing a child's learning and overall development cannot be overstated. This introduction highlights the significance of this involvement, focusing on how parents and caregivers can actively contribute to their child's learning journey, thereby enhancing learning outcomes, boosting child motivation, and strengthening the parent-child relationship.

One of the key strategies for engaging parents in game-based learning is effective communication about the benefits of educational games. Educators play a vital role in this, and this section offers strategies on how they can effectively convey the value of digital games in supporting various aspects of learning, from cognitive development to social skills. It also provides insights into addressing common parental concerns regarding screen time and digital game usage, emphasizing a balanced perspective on the educational merits of these tools.

Involving parents in the game selection process is essential to ensure the games align with educational goals, are age-appropriate, and hold educational value. This section discusses collaborative game selection and provides guidelines for establishing healthy screen time habits for children, including recommendations on the duration and monitoring of digital game interaction.

Digital games also offer a unique opportunity for enhancing parent-child interactions. This introduction explores how digital games can serve as tools for meaningful interaction, focusing on games that are suitable for cooperative play and those that encourage discussion and joint problem-solving. Furthermore, it offers ideas for activity-based learning, suggesting games and activities that parents can engage in with their children to enrich the learning experience and strengthen their bond.

Providing educational resources and support to parents is crucial to extend learning beyond the classroom. This section discusses the types of resources that schools and educators can provide to support game-based learning at home, such as recommended game lists, guides on playing these games with children, and tips for reinforcing learning outside the digital environment.

Lastly, the importance of creating parent support networks and communities is highlighted. This includes establishing online forums, organizing parent workshops, and facilitating school meetings where parents can share experiences, resources, and support each other in leveraging digital games for educational purposes.

In conclusion, this introduction underscores the critical role of parents and caregivers in supporting and enriching the game-based learning experience for preschoolers. By actively participating and collaborating in their child's digital gaming experience, parents and caregivers can significantly enhance the effectiveness of these educational tools, fostering an environment conducive to learning, growth, and meaningful engagement.

40

IMPORTANCE OF INVOLVING PARENTS AND CAREGIVERS IN PRESCHOOL EDUCATION

Involving parents and caregivers in preschool education is vital, as it fosters a supportive learning environment, strengthens the home-school connection, and enriches the child's educational experience through collaborative efforts.

Critical Role in Early Development

Parental involvement in the early stages of a child's education is not just beneficial; it's crucial. The role that parents and caregivers play during this foundational period can significantly shape a child's learning trajectory and overall development.

1. **Formative Influence**: Parents and caregivers are a child's first teachers. Their interactions, language use, and engagement in playful activities lay the groundwork for future learning and cognitive development. For instance, simple activities like reading bedtime stories or playing counting games can stimulate early literacy and numeracy skills.

2. **Emotional and Social Development**: The emotional support and secure environment provided by parents and caregivers contribute greatly to a child's social and emotional development. Children who feel supported and understood by their parents tend to have higher self-esteem and are better equipped to form healthy relationships with peers and adults.

3. **Modeling Learning Behavior**: Parents and caregivers model learning behavior and attitudes towards education. Children whose parents show an interest in learning activities, such as reading books or exploring nature, are more likely to develop a positive attitude toward learning and curiosity about the world.

Benefits of Parental Engagement

Engaging parents and caregivers in educational activities extends the learning environment beyond the classroom and provides numerous benefits:

1. **Enhanced Learning Outcomes**: When parents are involved in their child's education, it can lead to better learning outcomes. This involvement can range from helping with homework to engaging in educational activities at home, reinforcing and supplementing what is learned in school.

2. **Improved Motivation and Behavior**: Children whose parents are actively involved in their education often show higher levels of motivation and better behavior in school. Knowing that their educational efforts are valued at home can encourage children to engage more fully in school activities.

3. **Stronger Parent-Child Relationships**: Educational activities can strengthen the bond between parents and children. Working together on homework, playing educational games, or engaging in discussions about what was learned in school fosters mutual respect, understanding, and communication.

4. **Early Identification of Learning Challenges**: Parents who are involved in their child's education are more likely to notice if their child is facing learning challenges or developmental delays. Early identification allows for timely intervention and support.

5. **Cultural and Value-Based Education**: Parental involvement also means that children's learning can be supplemented with cultural education and value-based teachings that are important within the family. This can include teaching children about their cultural heritage, religious beliefs, or family values.

In conclusion, the involvement of parents and caregivers in preschool education is integral to a child's holistic development. It supports cognitive, social, emotional, and moral development, leading to a well-rounded and fulfilling educational experience. Engaging parents in the educational process not only benefits children but also enriches the family unit and strengthens the bond between parents and their children.

41

STRATEGIES FOR COMMUNICATING THE BENEFITS OF GAME-BASED LEARNING TO PARENTS

Communicating the benefits of game-based learning to parents involves highlighting its role in cognitive and skill development, providing evidence of educational outcomes, and demonstrating how it complements traditional learning methods. Effectively communicating the benefits of game-based learning to parents is crucial for gaining their support and involvement.

Here are several strategies educators can use:

Educational Workshops and Meetings

1. **Organize Informational Workshops**: Host workshops or information sessions for parents that focus on the educational benefits of game-based learning. Use these platforms to showcase how digital games can support various aspects of learning, such as cognitive development, language acquisition, and problem-solving skills.

2. **Demonstration Sessions**: Conduct demonstration sessions where parents can observe or participate in game-based learning activities. This hands-on experience can help parents understand how games are used in an educational context.

Clear and Effective Communication

1. **Use Simple, Jargon-Free Language**: When explaining the benefits of game-based learning to parents, use language that is easy to understand. Avoid educational jargon and focus on clear, relatable examples.

2. **Highlight Specific Educational Outcomes**: Provide specific examples of how game-based learning can improve educational outcomes. For instance, explain

how a particular game improves math skills or enhances language proficiency.

Providing Evidence and Research
1. **Share Research Findings**: Offer parents access to research studies or articles that highlight the positive impact of game-based learning. This evidence can help validate the use of digital games in an educational setting.

2. **Success Stories and Testimonials**: Share success stories or testimonials from other educators, parents, or students who have had positive experiences with game-based learning.

Involving Parents in the Process
1. **Parental Participation**: Invite parents to participate in game-based learning activities. This involvement can help them see firsthand how these games are beneficial for their children's education.

2. **Feedback Mechanisms**: Implement feedback mechanisms where parents can share their observations and concerns about their child's engagement with game-based learning. This can help in adjusting the approach to better suit individual student needs.

Utilizing Technology
1. **Online Platforms and Resources**: Use online platforms, such as school websites or educational blogs, to post information about game-based learning. This can include articles, infographics, or videos that explain the benefits and address common concerns.

2. **Virtual Demonstrations**: For parents who cannot attend in-person sessions, offer virtual demonstrations or webinars that showcase how game-based learning is implemented in the classroom.

Regular Updates and Communication
1. **Regular Newsletters or Emails**: Send out regular newsletters or emails to parents with updates on how game-based learning is being incorporated into the curriculum and the progress students are making.

1. **Parent-Teacher Meetings**: Use regular parent-teacher meetings to discuss the role of game-based learning in the child's education and provide updates on the child's progress and engagement.

By employing these strategies, educators can effectively communicate the benefits of game-based learning to parents, addressing their concerns and gaining their support. This can lead to a more collaborative and supportive learning environment that recognizes the value of integrating technology into education.

42

Involving Parents in Game Selection and Monitoring Screen Time

Involving parents in game selection and monitoring screen time ensures that digital play aligns with educational goals, is age-appropriate, and balances with other crucial aspects of childhood development.

Collaborative Game Selection

1. **Parental Involvement in Game Selection**: Encourage parents to be actively involved in selecting digital games for their children. This involvement ensures that the games align with the family's values, the child's interests, and educational goals.

2. **Assessing Educational Value**: Guide parents on how to assess the educational value of games. This involves looking for games that are not only entertaining but also contribute to the child's learning. For example, parents can choose games that teach math, language, or problem-solving skills.

3. **Checking Age-Appropriateness**: Advise parents to check the age appropriateness of games. This includes ensuring the content is suitable for the child's age and developmental stage. For example, games for preschoolers should avoid complex rules and should focus on basic concepts and skills.

4. **Alignment with Learning Objectives**: Help parents understand how to select games that align with specific learning objectives. For instance, if a child is learning about shapes, parents can choose games that involve shape recognition and sorting.

Guidelines for Screen Time

1. **Setting Time Limits**: Establish guidelines for how long children should engage with digital games. For preschoolers, recommend a balanced approach where digital game time does not exceed a recommended duration per day, in line with guidelines from pediatric organizations.

2. **Quality Over Quantity**: Emphasize the importance of focusing on the quality of screen time rather than just the quantity. Encourage parents to select high-quality, educational games that contribute to the child's learning and development.

3. **Creating a Screen Time Schedule**: Assist parents in creating a daily screen time schedule that allocates specific times for digital games. This schedule should also include ample time for other activities, such as physical play, reading, and family time.

4. **Active Monitoring and Involvement**: Encourage parents to actively monitor their child's screen time. This can involve co-playing games with the child, discussing the content of the games, and observing the child's behavior and reactions during and after gameplay.

5. **Encouraging Breaks and Diverse Activities**: Advise parents to encourage regular breaks from screen time to prevent excessive exposure. Additionally, suggest incorporating a variety of activities throughout the day to ensure a well-rounded routine that includes physical activity, creative play, and social interaction.

6. **Use of Parental Control Tools**: Inform parents about the availability of parental control tools and features that can help manage and monitor screen time. These tools can restrict game access during certain hours, limit overall daily screen time, and block inappropriate content.

Involving parents in the game selection process and establishing healthy screen time habits are crucial steps in ensuring a positive and productive digital gaming experience for children. By providing guidance and tools, educators can empower parents to make informed decisions that benefit their child's development and well-being.

43

Encouraging Parent-Child Interactions Through Digital Games

Encouraging parent-child interactions through digital games can deepen bonds, enhance learning experiences, and provide opportunities for parents to actively engage in their child's educational journey in a fun and interactive way.

Games as a Tool for Interaction

1. **Cooperative Play Games**: Encourage parents to engage in digital games that are designed for cooperative play. These games require players to work together to achieve common goals, making them ideal for fostering teamwork and communication between parents and children. For instance, puzzle-solving games like "Snipperclips" or "Pode" where players need to collaborate to solve puzzles can be enjoyable and bonding experiences.

2. **Discussion-Prompting Games**: Some games are specifically designed to prompt discussion and decision-making, which can be great for parent-child interaction. Games that present moral dilemmas or require players to make choices together, like "Minecraft: Story Mode," can lead to meaningful conversations and shared decision-making experiences.

3. **Educational and Trivia Games**: Games that involve trivia or learning new facts can be both fun and educational for families. For example, quiz games like "Trivia Crack" or "Kahoot!" can be played together, with parents and children learning and testing their knowledge in various subjects.

Activity-Based Learning

1. **Real-World Activities Linked to Game Content**: Suggest games that have real-world activity counterparts. For instance, if a child plays a cooking game, parents can follow up with an actual cooking session, helping to apply what the child learned in the game to a real-life context.

2. **Physical Activity Games**: Recommend games that encourage physical activity, which parents and children can do together. This can include motion-controlled games or fitness games that involve dancing, sports, or yoga. These activities not only promote physical health but also provide fun ways for families to engage together.

3. **Creative and Building Games**: Games that involve building or creating, such as "Lego Worlds" or "Toca Builders," can inspire similar real-world creative activities. After playing such games, parents and children can engage in arts and crafts, building models, or drawing, mirroring the creative processes in the game.

4. **Exploration and Adventure Games**: Suggest exploration-based games that can inspire outdoor activities. For example, a game focused on nature exploration can lead to a family hiking trip or a nature scavenger hunt, encouraging exploration and learning about the environment.

5. **Storytelling and Role-Playing Games**: Role-playing games where players create stories or characters can be great for imaginative play outside the digital world. Parents and children can create stories, dress up, and act out scenarios, enhancing creativity and storytelling skills.

By incorporating these types of games and activities into their routines, parents can use digital games as a springboard for meaningful, educational, and fun interactions with their children. This approach not only enhances the learning experience but also strengthens the parent-child bond through shared activities and interests.

44

RESOURCES AND SUPPORT FOR PARENTS TO EXTEND LEARNING BEYOND THE CLASSROOM

Providing resources and support for parents to extend learning beyond the classroom includes offering educational materials, suggesting activities that reinforce classroom concepts, and guiding them on how to create enriching learning environments at home.

Providing Educational Resources

1. **Lists of Recommended Games**: Schools and educators can provide parents with curated lists of educational games that are age-appropriate and align with learning objectives. These lists can include a variety of games focusing on different subjects, such as math, language arts, science, and social studies. For instance, a list could include games like "DragonBox" for math learning and "Endless Alphabet" for literacy skills.

2. **Guides on Game Usage**: Along with game recommendations, providing guides on how to effectively use these games can be highly beneficial. These guides can offer tips on integrating game play into daily routines, using games to reinforce concepts learned in school, and balancing game time with other activities.

3. **Tips for Reinforcing Learning**: Educators can offer tips and strategies for parents to reinforce the learning that occurs in game-based environments. This might include conversation starters related to game content, activities that complement the games, or ideas for applying game concepts to real-world scenarios.

1. **Customized Learning Plans**: For more personalized support, educators can help parents create customized learning plans that incorporate digital games. These plans can outline specific learning goals, suggest appropriate games, and provide a schedule that balances educational screen time with other learning activities.

Support Networks and Communities

1. **Online Parent Forums**: Establishing online forums or social media groups where parents can discuss game-based learning can be a valuable resource. These platforms allow parents to share experiences, ask questions, provide recommendations, and offer support to one another.

2. **Parent Workshops and Webinars**: Organizing workshops or webinars can help educate parents about the benefits and best practices of game-based learning. These sessions can cover a range of topics, from selecting educational games to integrating them effectively into children's learning routines.

3. **School Meetings and Discussions**: Regular school meetings or discussion groups focused on digital learning can foster a community of support. These meetings can serve as a platform for educators to share updates on educational technology, introduce new game-based learning tools, and gather feedback from parents.

4. **Collaboration with Game Developers**: Schools and educators can collaborate with game developers to provide insights into educational needs and preferences. This collaboration can lead to the creation of games that are more aligned with educational goals and more engaging for students.

5. **Resource Sharing Events**: Hosting events where parents can come together to share resources, such as game recommendations or educational apps, can build a supportive community. These events can also include swap sessions where parents exchange games and learning materials.

By providing these resources and fostering support networks, educators can empower parents to extend game-based learning beyond the classroom. This collaborative approach ensures that children receive a consistent and enriched learning experience, leveraging the benefits of digital games to enhance their education.

Overcoming Challenges and Addressing Concerns

In the dynamic landscape of early childhood education, the integration of digital games brings with it a range of challenges and concerns. This introduction sets the stage for a comprehensive exploration of these challenges and offers practical strategies for overcoming them, ensuring a positive and productive use of digital games in preschool settings.

A primary concern in using digital games in preschool education revolves around screen time and its developmental impact. Fears about attention span, physical activity levels, and an overreliance on technology for entertainment are common among educators and parents. This section will delve into these concerns, providing a balanced view of the impact of screen time on young children's development.

Another crucial aspect is content appropriateness. Ensuring that the digital games used in preschool are age-appropriate and offer educational value is paramount. This introduction explores the challenges in selecting suitable content and the importance of aligning games with educational objectives and developmental needs.

Managing screen time and ensuring the appropriate use of technology are key strategies in addressing these challenges. This includes balancing digital game time with other essential activities such as physical play, traditional learning methods, and social interactions. Recommendations for setting healthy screen time limits based on age and development needs will also be provided.

Overcoming resource limitations and resistance from stakeholders are significant barriers to implementing game-based learning. This section discusses strategies for addressing these challenges, including finding solutions for limited access to technology and budget constraints, as well as addressing skepticism from parents, educators, and administrators.

Supporting professional development for teachers is crucial in effectively using digital games in education. This includes training workshops, ongoing support, and the creation of educator networks and forums for sharing best practices, resources, and experiences.

Ensuring digital safety and addressing ethical considerations are also critical. Strategies for protecting children from inappropriate content and online risks, addressing data privacy issues, and considering the commercialization of educational tools will be explored. Additionally, the importance of using culturally sensitive and inclusive games that represent diverse backgrounds and experiences will be emphasized.

Exploring international trends and practices in digital game-based learning offers valuable insights. This section will look at how different countries and educational systems are integrating digital games in early childhood education, highlighting global trends and diverse approaches.

Finally, a roadmap for technology integration for schools and educators will be provided. This will include a step-by-step guide for integrating digital games into the curriculum, covering stages of adoption, necessary resources, and evaluation methods. Looking ahead at future trends and evolving technologies, this section will also discuss how educators can prepare for and adapt to these changes.

In conclusion, this introduction aims to address the various challenges and concerns associated with using digital games in preschool education, offering practical strategies and insights for educators and parents. By tackling these issues head-on, stakeholders can ensure that digital games are used effectively and responsibly to enhance early childhood learning experiences.

45

COMMON CHALLENGES AND CONCERNS RELATED TO USING DIGITAL GAMES IN PRESCHOOL

Common challenges and concerns related to using digital games in preschool include ensuring age-appropriateness, managing screen time effectively, balancing digital and physical play, and addressing potential overreliance on technology for learning.

Screen Time and Developmental Impact

1. **Impact on Attention Span**: One of the primary concerns regarding screen time is its potential impact on young children's attention spans. Prolonged exposure to fast-paced digital content can affect a child's ability to concentrate on slower-paced or less stimulating activities. This concern highlights the need for a balanced approach to screen time, where digital activities are interspersed with non-digital, concentration-building activities like reading or puzzle-solving.

2. **Physical Activity Levels**: Excessive screen time can lead to sedentary behavior, reducing the time children spend on physical activities essential for their physical development. It's crucial to balance digital game play with ample opportunities for active play, such as outdoor games, sports, and other forms of exercise.

3. **Overreliance on Technology for Entertainment**: There's a risk of children becoming overly reliant on digital devices for entertainment, potentially impacting their ability to engage in imaginative play or find enjoyment in non-digital activities. Encouraging a variety of play experiences, including unstructured and imaginative play, can mitigate this risk.

1. **Social Interaction and Emotional Development**: Excessive screen time can also impact social and emotional development, especially if it replaces face-to-face interactions and collaborative play with peers. It's important to encourage social activities and playdates that foster interpersonal skills.

Content Appropriateness
1. **Age-Appropriate Content**: Ensuring that the content of digital games is age-appropriate for preschoolers is crucial. This includes not only avoiding content that is overtly inappropriate for young children but also ensuring that the complexity of the game is suited to their developmental stage. Games should be easily understandable and playable for young children.

2. **Educational Value**: Parents and educators should evaluate digital games for their educational value. Ideally, games used in preschool settings should support learning objectives, whether they're teaching specific skills like numeracy or literacy, or broader cognitive skills like problem-solving and memory.

3. **Cultural Sensitivity and Inclusivity**: Games should be evaluated for cultural sensitivity and inclusivity, ensuring they represent diverse backgrounds and do not perpetuate stereotypes. This helps in providing a well-rounded perspective and promotes acceptance and understanding from a young age.

4. **Commercial Content and Advertising**: Another aspect to consider is the presence of commercial content and advertising within games. Games aimed at children should ideally be free of advertisements, as young children might not distinguish between the game content and commercial messages.

By addressing these common concerns and challenges, educators and parents can create a more balanced and effective approach to using digital games in preschool settings. This approach involves not just selecting appropriate content but also balancing screen time with a variety of other activities that contribute to a child's holistic development.

46

STRATEGIES FOR MANAGING SCREEN TIME AND ENSURING APPROPRIATE USE OF TECHNOLOGY

Managing screen time and ensuring appropriate use of technology involves setting clear time limits, choosing educational and age-appropriate content, integrating technology with other learning activities, and actively engaging with children during screen use.

Balancing Screen Time with Other Activities

1. **Creating a Diverse Activity Schedule**: Encourage a daily schedule that balances digital game time with a variety of other activities. This schedule can include physical play, arts and crafts, reading time, and interactive play with peers or family members. For example, after a 30-minute session with an educational game, children could engage in an hour of outdoor play or a creative art project.

2. **Integrating Technology with Learning**: Use technology as a tool to complement traditional learning methods rather than replace them. Digital games can be integrated into lesson plans as a supplementary tool, followed by hands-on activities that reinforce the concepts learned digitally.

3. **Encouraging Family Participation**: Promote activities where the whole family can participate. This can include board games, outdoor sports, or family walks, which offer opportunities for social interaction and physical exercise, providing a healthy counterbalance to screen time.

4. **Promoting Unstructured Play**: Unstructured play is crucial for a child's development. Encourage periods where children can engage in free play, using

their imagination and creativity without the influence of technology.

Guidelines for Screen Time

1. **Establishing Daily Limits**: Set clear guidelines for the amount of time children can spend on digital devices each day. For preschoolers, organizations like the American Academy of Pediatrics (AAP) recommend no more than 1 hour of high-quality programming per day.

2. **Quality Over Quantity**: Focus on the quality of screen time rather than just the quantity. Opt for educational games and content that contribute to a child's learning and development, avoiding passive screen activities like prolonged video watching.

3. **Setting Tech-Free Zones and Times**: Create tech-free zones in the home, such as the dining area or bedrooms, and establish tech-free times, especially during family meals and before bedtime. This can help in reducing screen dependence and improving sleep quality.

4. **Monitoring and Discussing Content**: Actively monitor the content of the games and apps that children are using. Discuss the content with them to ensure they understand and are getting the most out of their screen time.

5. **Educational Screen Time Prioritization**: Prioritize screen time that is educational and interactive over passive screen use. Choose games and apps that are interactive, engaging, and provide some form of learning or skill development.

6. **Regular Breaks and Eye Care**: Encourage regular breaks from screen time to prevent eye strain. Teach children to practice the 20-20-20 rule: every 20 minutes, look away from the screen and focus on something 20 feet away for 20 seconds.

7. **Parental Control and Monitoring Tools**: Utilize parental control tools to help manage and monitor children's screen time. These tools can limit access to certain apps, set time limits, and provide reports on screen time usage.

By implementing these strategies, parents and educators can manage screen time effectively, ensuring that children benefit from technology while also engaging in a range of other developmental activities. Balancing digital interaction with physical, social, and creative experiences is key to fostering a well-rounded upbringing in the digital age.

47

ADDRESSING POTENTIAL BARRIERS TO IMPLEMENTING GAME-BASED LEARNING

Addressing potential barriers to implementing game-based learning includes navigating resource limitations, ensuring equitable access to technology, providing training for educators, and overcoming skepticism about the educational value of digital games.

Resource Limitations

1. **Creative Utilization of Available Technology**: In cases where the latest technology isn't available, focus on creatively using whatever resources are at hand. For instance, older computers or tablets can still run many educational games effectively. It's more about how the technology is used rather than having the latest model.

2. **Seeking Community and Corporate Partnerships**: Schools can reach out to local businesses or community organizations for partnerships. These entities might be willing to donate equipment or provide funding for technology resources. This collaboration can be mutually beneficial, offering publicity and community goodwill for the businesses involved.

3. **Crowdfunding and Grants**: Consider crowdfunding platforms or educational grants specifically aimed at integrating technology into classrooms. There are numerous organizations and initiatives that support educational technology integration, and tapping into these resources can provide much-needed funding.

1. **Shared Device Models**: Implement a shared device model in classrooms, where students take turns using available technology. While not ideal, this can still provide students with regular access to digital learning tools.

Resistance from Stakeholders

1. **Educational Workshops for Stakeholders**: Organize workshops or information sessions to educate stakeholders about the benefits of game-based learning. These sessions can showcase how digital games can enhance learning, backed by research and case studies.

2. **Pilot Programs and Demonstrations**: Start with pilot programs in selected classes or subjects to demonstrate the effectiveness of game-based learning. Share the results and feedback from these pilots with stakeholders to showcase the tangible benefits.

3. **Involving Stakeholders in the Selection Process**: Involve parents, educators, and administrators in the game selection process. This inclusion can help address concerns about content appropriateness and educational value.

4. **Addressing Concerns Directly**: Openly discuss the concerns of stakeholders. For example, if parents are worried about screen time, explain how game-based learning is balanced with other non-digital activities in the curriculum.

5. **Highlighting Success Stories and Best Practices**: Share success stories and best practices from other schools or districts where game-based learning has been successfully implemented. This can help alleviate fears and show the potential of digital games in education.

6. **Regular Updates and Transparency**: Keep stakeholders regularly informed about the implementation of game-based learning, the outcomes, and the ongoing adjustments based on feedback. Transparency in the process can build trust and support.

By addressing resource limitations creatively and tackling resistance through education, demonstration, and inclusion, schools can effectively overcome barriers to implementing game-based learning. These strategies require a combination of resourcefulness, open communication, and a focus on demonstrating the tangible benefits of digital games in education.

48

SUPPORTING PROFESSIONAL DEVELOPMENT FOR TEACHERS IN USING DIGITAL GAMES

Supporting professional development for teachers in using digital games involves offering training workshops, sharing best practices, providing access to educational technology resources, and fostering a collaborative environment for sharing experiences and insights.

Training and Workshops

1. **Specialized Training Sessions**: Organize training sessions for teachers that focus on the effective integration of digital games into the curriculum. These sessions can cover various aspects, from selecting appropriate games to using them as effective teaching tools. For example, a workshop could demonstrate how to use a math game to reinforce arithmetic skills.

2. **Ongoing Support and Development**: Provide ongoing support to educators after initial training sessions. This could include regular follow-up meetings or access to a help desk where teachers can get assistance with any challenges they encounter in using digital games in their classrooms.

3. **Incorporating Pedagogical Techniques**: Training should also focus on how to blend traditional pedagogical techniques with digital game-based learning. For instance, teachers can learn how to use games as part of a larger lesson plan that includes discussions, hands-on activities, and other teaching methods.

4. **Customized Workshops Based on Skill Levels**: Offer workshops tailored to different skill levels, from beginners to advanced users, so that all teachers can

benefit, regardless of their prior experience with digital technology.

Best Practices and Resource Sharing

1. **Educator Networks and Online Forums**: Create or leverage existing educator networks and online forums where teachers can share experiences, resources, and insights about using digital games in teaching. This collaborative environment can be a valuable source of support and inspiration.

2. **Sharing Success Stories and Challenges**: Encourage teachers to share their success stories and challenges in these networks. For example, a teacher could share how a particular game helped improve student engagement in a challenging subject.

3. **Resource Database**: Develop or contribute to a shared database of resources, including game recommendations, lesson plans, and integration strategies. This database could be accessible to all educators within a school district or a broader educational community.

4. **Collaborative Learning Communities**: Facilitate the formation of learning communities among teachers focused on game-based learning. These groups can meet regularly to discuss new ideas, troubleshoot issues, and brainstorm innovative ways to integrate digital games into teaching.

5. **Webinars and Online Training Resources**: Provide access to webinars and online training modules for teachers who cannot attend in-person workshops. These online resources offer flexibility and can cover a wide range of topics related to digital game-based learning.

By investing in professional development and fostering a culture of collaboration and resource sharing, schools and educational institutions can empower teachers to effectively utilize digital games in their teaching. This support not only enhances teachers' skills and confidence in using digital tools but also enriches the overall learning experience for students.

49

DIGITAL SAFETY, ETHICS, AND CULTURAL SENSITIVITY IN GAME-BASED LEARNING

Ensuring digital safety, ethics, and cultural sensitivity in game-based learning requires careful selection of content, educating children about online safety, fostering an inclusive environment, and respecting diverse backgrounds and perspectives.

Ensuring Digital Safety

1. **Content Filtering and Monitoring**: Implement content filters and monitoring tools to prevent children from accessing inappropriate content. Educators and parents should be familiar with the digital games' content, ensuring it aligns with age-appropriate standards.

2. **Safe Online Interactions**: Teach children about safe online behaviors, particularly in games that offer multiplayer or social networking features. Strategies include creating anonymous profiles, understanding the importance of not sharing personal information, and recognizing inappropriate conversations or behaviors.

3. **Parental Controls**: Educate parents about using parental controls available in most digital devices and gaming platforms. These controls can restrict game downloads, limit online interactions, and monitor game usage.

4. **Regular Reviews of Game Content**: Continuously review and assess game content to ensure it remains appropriate, especially as online games can be updated with new content regularly.

Ethical Considerations
1. **Data Privacy and Protection**: Address the importance of data privacy in digital games. Ensure that any game used in educational settings complies with laws and regulations regarding children's data, such as the Children's Online Privacy Protection Act (COPPA).

2. **Commercialization Concerns**: Be aware of the commercialization of educational tools. Choose games that are free of advertisements and in-game purchases, especially for younger children, to avoid commercial influences and unintentional spending.

3. **Transparent Usage of Data**: If a game collects data on student performance, ensure transparency about how this data is used and stored. Parents and educators should be informed about data collection practices and give consent where necessary.

Cultural Sensitivity and Inclusivity
1. **Diverse Representation in Games**: Select games that offer diverse and inclusive representations. This includes characters with various ethnicities, cultures, abilities, and backgrounds, ensuring that all children can see themselves represented in the games they play.

2. **Culturally Relevant Content**: Choose games with content that respects and reflects a wide range of cultures and lifestyles. This could include games that explore different cultural stories, traditions, and languages.

3. **Avoiding Cultural Stereotypes**: Be vigilant about games that may perpetuate cultural stereotypes. Games should be evaluated not only for educational content but also for how they portray different cultures and groups.

4. **Encouraging Cultural Awareness and Respect**: Utilize games as a tool to teach and encourage cultural awareness and respect. Games that involve learning about different cultures or working collaboratively with diverse groups can promote understanding and inclusivity.

By addressing digital safety, ethical considerations, and cultural sensitivity, educators and parents can ensure a safe, respectful, and inclusive environment for children engaging in game-based learning. This approach not only protects children but also fosters an educational space that respects and celebrates diversity and ethical practices.

50

GLOBAL PERSPECTIVES ON DIGITAL GAME-BASED LEARNING

Exploring global perspectives on digital game-based learning reveals diverse approaches and attitudes, highlighting how cultural, educational, and technological differences shape the integration and impact of digital games in various educational settings worldwide.

International Trends and Practices
1. **Adoption of Educational Technologies**: Different countries have embraced digital game-based learning to varying degrees. For instance, in countries like South Korea and Japan, there is a strong emphasis on integrating technology into early childhood education, with games focusing on both academic subjects and social skills.

2. **Cultural Influences in Game Design**: In regions like Scandinavia, there's a focus on games that promote creativity and collaborative learning, reflecting cultural values that emphasize teamwork and innovation. Scandinavian educational games often feature open-ended gameplay and encourage exploration and problem-solving.

3. **Government Initiatives and Funding**: Some countries have government-led initiatives or funding programs to support the development and integration of educational games. For example, in the United States, programs like the Small Business Innovation Research (SBIR) grants have funded the development of innovative educational games and technologies.

4. **Public-Private Partnerships**: In places like Singapore and the UK, there are instances of public-private partnerships to create and implement educational gaming platforms, leveraging the expertise of tech companies and educational specialists.

Learning from Global Practices

1. **Diverse Educational Approaches**: Understanding how different cultures and countries use digital games in education can provide a wealth of ideas and approaches. For example, educators can learn from Asian countries about integrating technology into early learning, or from European models that emphasize creativity and problem-solving.

2. **Cross-Cultural Collaboration**: Collaborating with international educators and game developers can lead to the creation of more diverse and inclusive educational games. These collaborations can bring together various cultural perspectives and educational philosophies, leading to games that are more globally relevant and accessible.

3. **Sharing Success Stories and Challenges**: By examining the successes and challenges faced by educators in different parts of the world, valuable lessons can be learned. For instance, learning from a country where digital game-based learning has significantly improved student engagement can provide insights into effective implementation strategies.

4. **Adapting Global Innovations to Local Contexts**: Educators can adapt the innovative practices and technologies used in other countries to their local educational contexts. This adaptation should consider cultural differences and local educational needs to ensure relevance and effectiveness.

5. **Global Standards and Frameworks**: Understanding global trends can also help in aligning local educational practices with international standards and frameworks, ensuring that students are receiving a globally competitive education.

In conclusion, exploring global perspectives on digital game-based learning provides valuable insights into diverse educational practices and technological innovations. By learning from these international experiences, educators can enrich their own teaching practices, enhance the cultural relevance of their educational tools, and ensure their approaches align with global trends and standards.

51

TECHNOLOGY INTEGRATION ROADMAP FOR SCHOOLS AND EDUCATORS

Creating a technology integration roadmap for schools and educators involves assessing current resources, setting clear objectives, providing training and support, and continuously evaluating the effectiveness of technology in enhancing the educational experience.

Step-by-Step Integration Guide

1. **Assessment and Planning**: Begin by assessing the current technological capabilities and educational needs of the school. This includes understanding the available hardware, software, and the skills level of educators and students. Develop a plan that outlines the goals for integrating digital games, including which subjects or skills will be targeted.

2. **Training and Professional Development**: Prioritize training for educators. This could involve workshops, online courses, or collaboration with tech-savvy teachers. The focus should be on both technical skills and pedagogical strategies for integrating games into teaching.

3. **Pilot Testing**: Start with pilot programs in selected classes. Choose digital games that align with the curriculum and evaluate their effectiveness. Feedback from these pilots can guide broader implementation.

4. **Full-Scale Implementation**: Based on the success of the pilots, gradually implement digital game-based learning across the school. This phase should involve regular monitoring and support for teachers.

5. **Continuous Evaluation and Feedback**: Establish mechanisms for ongoing evaluation of the program. This includes collecting feedback from teachers, students, and parents, and regularly assessing student performance and engagement.

6. **Adjustments and Scaling**: Use the feedback and evaluation data to make necessary adjustments. Scale the successful practices to more classes and grades within the school.

Future Trends and Evolving Technology

1. **Augmented and Virtual Reality**: Stay abreast of developments in AR and VR. These technologies are becoming more accessible and have the potential to provide immersive and interactive learning experiences. Schools should consider how these tools can be integrated into the curriculum.

2. **Artificial Intelligence**: AI is poised to transform educational gaming with personalized learning experiences. Educators should explore how AI-driven games can be used to adapt to individual student's learning paces and styles.

3. **Internet of Things (IoT) and Connectivity**: With the growth of IoT, physical and digital learning environments will become more interconnected. Educators should consider how IoT devices can enhance learning, such as through interactive classroom tools that integrate with educational games.

4. **Data Analytics**: Data-driven teaching will play a significant role in education. Understanding how to interpret data from digital games to inform teaching strategies and personalize learning will be crucial.

5. **Preparing for Continuous Change**: Emphasize the importance of a mindset geared towards continuous learning and adaptation among educators. As technology evolves rapidly, educators need to be flexible and open to adopting new tools and methods.

6. **Digital Literacy and Citizenship**: As digital games become an integral part of learning, teaching digital literacy and responsible digital citizenship will become increasingly important. Educators should incorporate these aspects into their digital game-based learning initiatives.

By following this roadmap, schools and educators can effectively integrate digital games into their curriculum and stay prepared for future technological advancements. This approach ensures that students are not only engaged and motivated but also equipped with the skills to navigate and succeed in a rapidly changing digital world.

FUTURE TRENDS AND CONSIDERATIONS IN INTERACTIVE DIGITAL GAMES FOR EARLY LEARNING

As we navigate the rapidly evolving landscape of early childhood education, interactive digital games stand at the forefront of educational innovation. This introduction delves into the future trends and considerations in using interactive digital games for early learning, exploring how emerging technologies and pedagogical advancements are shaping the next generation of educational experiences.

At the cutting edge of educational technology are developments like augmented reality (AR), virtual reality (VR), and artificial intelligence (AI). These technologies are revolutionizing the way digital games are used in learning, offering immersive and interactive experiences that were previously unimaginable. This section will explore how these advancements are influencing digital game-based learning and the potential they hold for the future of education.

Another significant trend is the gamification of education. This approach involves integrating game design elements into educational settings to make learning more engaging and interactive. This section will discuss how gamification is being applied in early learning environments and the impact it has on student engagement and motivation.

Personalization and adaptive learning are also gaining traction, offering tailored educational experiences that meet the unique needs and learning paces of individual children. This trend towards customized learning is facilitated by adaptive technology that can modify content in real-time based on the learner's performance and preferences.

Innovations in interactive game design are also transforming the user experience (UX) for young learners. This includes designing intuitive interfaces and child-friendly graphics that make digital games more accessible and enjoyable for preschool-age children. Additionally, modern game design is increasingly incorporating educational theories, such as constructivism and inquiry-based learning, to create more effective and meaningful learning experiences.

The integration of digital games in education is also leading to shifts in teaching methodologies and classroom dynamics. Emerging technologies are influencing the adoption of blended learning environments, where digital games are combined with traditional teaching methods. This section will explore how these shifts are changing the role of teachers and educators, emphasizing the need for ongoing professional development and adaptability in a tech-enhanced learning landscape.

Looking forward, it is crucial to prepare for future advancements and challenges in digital game-based learning. This includes staying abreast of rapid technological developments, addressing the digital divide to ensure equitable access to learning opportunities, and being vigilant about ethical and privacy concerns associated with advanced educational technologies.

Finally, fostering a culture of continuous learning and innovation among educators, parents, and policymakers is essential to fully leverage the benefits of digital games in early education. This section will emphasize the importance of embracing change and innovation to enrich learning experiences and prepare young learners for a future that is increasingly intertwined with technology.

In conclusion, this introduction provides a glimpse into the future of interactive digital games in early learning, highlighting the exciting possibilities and considerations that lie ahead. By embracing these emerging trends and preparing for the challenges they bring, educators and parents can ensure that digital games continue to be a valuable and impactful tool in the education of young learners.

52

Emerging Trends in Educational Technology and Digital Games

Emerging trends in educational technology and digital games include personalized learning experiences, augmented and virtual reality applications, adaptive learning algorithms, and an increased focus on developing soft skills and emotional intelligence through interactive gameplay.

Advancements in Educational Technology

1. **Augmented Reality (AR)**: AR in education offers an interactive experience where digital elements are overlaid in the real world. For example, AR can be used to bring historical figures to life in a classroom, or to illustrate complex scientific processes in a visually engaging manner. Apps like "Augment Education" allow students to interact with 3D models, enhancing their understanding of abstract concepts.

2. **Virtual Reality (VR)**: VR provides an immersive learning experience, allowing students to explore virtual environments. For instance, VR can transport students to different geographical locations, historical periods, or even inside the human body. Tools like "Google Expeditions" enable these immersive educational journeys, making learning more engaging and experiential.

3. **Artificial Intelligence (AI)**: AI in education is revolutionizing personalized learning. AI algorithms can analyze a student's performance and adapt the curriculum to their learning style and pace. This results in a highly customized learning experience, with platforms like "Carnegie Learning" providing AI-driven learning paths.

Gamification of Education

1. **Incorporating Game Mechanics in Learning**: The trend of gamification involves using game design elements in educational contexts. This includes elements like points, badges, leaderboards, and progress tracking to motivate and engage students. For example, platforms like "ClassDojo" use points and rewards to encourage positive student behavior.

2. **Story-Based Learning**: Integrating narrative elements into educational content can make learning more compelling. Digital games with storylines where students need to solve problems or complete tasks to progress in the story are becoming increasingly popular. These stories can be tailored to suit educational content across various subjects.

3. **Competition and Collaboration**: Gamification also includes fostering healthy competition and collaboration among students. Tools like "Kahoot!" turn learning into a fun and competitive game, encouraging participation and engagement.

Personalization and Adaptive Learning

1. **Adaptive Learning Platforms**: These platforms assess individual student performance and adapt in real-time to provide personalized learning experiences. For example, "DreamBox Learning" offers adaptive math lessons, where the difficulty level and content are automatically adjusted to meet each student's needs.

2. **Learning Analytics**: The use of analytics in education enables teachers to track student progress and identify areas where students might need additional support. This data-driven approach allows for more targeted and effective teaching strategies.

3. **Interactive and Responsive Content**: Digital games and learning platforms are increasingly becoming interactive and responsive to student inputs. This interactivity ensures that the learning experience is engaging and tailored to the individual learner's responses and choices.

These emerging trends in educational technology and digital games are transforming traditional educational models, making learning more engaging, personalized, and effective. By leveraging these advancements, educators can provide students with rich, interactive, and customized learning experiences that meet the needs of diverse learners in a rapidly evolving digital age.

53

Innovations in Interactive Game Design for Early Learning

Innovations in interactive game design for early learning are focusing on immersive experiences, intuitive interfaces tailored for young learners, integration of augmented reality for enhanced engagement, and adaptive learning paths that personalize educational content.

User Experience (UX) for Young Learners

1. **Intuitive Interfaces**: Modern game design for young learners focuses on creating interfaces that are intuitive and easy to navigate. This includes large, colorful buttons, simple menus, and drag-and-drop functionalities. For example, games like "Toca Boca" use vibrant, visually appealing interfaces that are easy for young children to understand and interact with.

2. **Child-Friendly Graphics and Animations**: The aesthetic design of games is tailored to appeal to young learners. This involves the use of bright colors, simple shapes, and engaging animations. Games like "Peg + Cat: The Big Dog Problem" use cartoon-style graphics and animations to captivate and maintain the attention of young children.

3. **Interactive Feedback and Encouragement**: Games designed for early learners often include interactive feedback mechanisms that encourage and guide the child. This could be in the form of an animated character that congratulates the child for completing a task or gently guides them if they make a mistake.

1. **Touchscreen Adaptability**: Recognizing that young children are often more adept at using touchscreens, many games are designed with touchscreen play in mind. This includes gestures that are natural to children, like swiping and tapping.

Incorporating Educational Theories

1. **Constructivism in Game Design**: Modern educational games are increasingly designed based on constructivist principles, where learning is seen as an active, constructive process. Games that encourage exploration, experimentation, and making connections between different concepts cater to this approach. For instance, a game that allows children to build their own virtual worlds can help them understand spatial relationships and basic physics.

2. **Inquiry-Based Learning**: Games that promote inquiry-based learning encourage children to ask questions, explore, and discover. For example, science games that simulate experiments or exploration games where children have to solve mysteries can enhance critical thinking and curiosity.

3. **Social-Emotional Learning (SEL)**: Games are also being designed to support SEL, teaching skills like empathy, cooperation, and emotional regulation. Games that involve role-playing or decision-making can help children practice and develop these important skills.

Cross-Curricular Learning Games

1. **Integration of Multiple Subjects**: Cross-curricular games combine elements from different subject areas, providing a more integrated and holistic learning experience. For example, a game might combine math and science by having children measure and mix ingredients in a virtual cooking activity.

2. **Thematic Learning Approaches**: Games that are based around themes or stories can naturally integrate multiple subject areas. A game set in space, for example, might include elements of astronomy, physics, and math, as well as language skills for reading and following instructions.

3. **Real-World Problem-Solving**: Some games simulate real-world problems that require knowledge from various domains. These games can teach children how different subjects intersect in real-life contexts, such as a game where they plan

and build a sustainable city, integrating environmental science, math, and social studies.

Innovations in interactive game design for early learning are focusing on making games more accessible, educational, and engaging for young learners. By incorporating thoughtful UX designs, educational theories, and cross-curricular approaches, these games are evolving to provide rich, multifaceted learning experiences that cater to the developmental needs and curiosities of young children.

54

ANTICIPATING CHANGES IN PRESCHOOL EDUCATION LANDSCAPES

Anticipating changes in the preschool education landscape involves staying attuned to advancements in educational technology, evolving pedagogical approaches, increasing emphasis on social-emotional learning, and adapting to the diverse needs of a new generation of learners.

Shifts in Teaching Methodologies

1. **Technology-Driven Interactive Learning**: Emerging technologies and digital games are leading to more interactive and student-centered learning approaches. Traditional lecture-based methods are giving way to more hands-on, exploratory learning experiences. For instance, a game that teaches numbers might involve interactive counting and sorting activities, rather than rote memorization.

2. **Differentiated Instruction**: Digital games enable teachers to more easily implement differentiated instruction, adapting teaching methods and materials to meet the varied needs of students. Games with adaptive learning capabilities can automatically adjust their difficulty level to suit each child's learning pace and style.

3. **Increased Collaboration and Group Learning**: The use of digital games often encourages collaborative learning. Teachers are now facilitating more group work and peer-to-peer learning, with games that require teamwork or group problem-solving.

1. **Data-Driven Instruction**: Emerging technologies provide teachers with real-time data on student performance and engagement. This data can inform instructional strategies, allowing teachers to tailor their approach to the needs of individual students.

Blended Learning Environments

1. **Combining Digital and Traditional Methods**: The future of preschool education is likely to see a more integrated approach to learning, combining digital games with traditional teaching methods. For example, a lesson on shapes might begin with a digital game for identification and sorting, followed by a hands-on activity like drawing or constructing shapes.

2. **Enhanced Engagement and Motivation**: Blended learning environments leverage the engaging aspects of digital games to enhance student motivation. Traditional activities can be gamified to make them more appealing, such as turning a science experiment into a quest or challenge.

3. **Flexibility and Accessibility**: Blended learning offers greater flexibility, allowing children to engage with learning materials at their own pace, both in the classroom and at home. This approach also makes learning more accessible, catering to different learning preferences and abilities.

Role of Teachers and Educators

1. **Facilitators of Learning**: In a tech-enhanced landscape, the role of teachers is evolving from traditional instructors to facilitators of learning. Teachers guide students through their learning journey, helping them navigate digital platforms and encouraging exploration and discovery.

2. **Continuous Professional Development**: To keep up with technological advancements, ongoing professional development is essential for teachers. This includes training in new educational technologies, digital game-based learning, and evolving pedagogical approaches.

3. **Adaptability and Innovation**: Teachers and educators need to be adaptable, embracing new technologies and methodologies. This adaptability extends to experimenting with innovative teaching practices and continually seeking ways to integrate technology in meaningful and effective ways.

4. **Collaboration with Tech Experts**: Educators are increasingly collaborating with technology experts, game designers, and educational researchers to develop and implement effective digital learning tools. This collaboration ensures that educational technologies are pedagogically sound and meet the specific needs of preschool learners.

As we anticipate changes in the preschool education landscape, it's clear that emerging technologies and digital games will play a significant role. These changes will require shifts in teaching methodologies, the adoption of blended learning environments, and a transformation in the role of teachers and educators. By embracing these changes, educators can provide a more dynamic, engaging, and personalized learning experience for young children.

55

PREPARING FOR FUTURE ADVANCEMENTS AND CHALLENGES IN DIGITAL GAME-BASED LEARNING

Preparing for future advancements and challenges in digital game-based learning requires continuous professional development, embracing adaptive and inclusive technologies, fostering resilience to rapidly changing educational environments, and proactively addressing ethical and accessibility concerns.

Staying Ahead of Technological Advancements

1. **Continuous Professional Development**: Educators and institutions should engage in continuous professional development to stay updated with the latest technological advancements. This can include attending tech-focused educational conferences, participating in online webinars, and subscribing to relevant educational technology journals or newsletters.

2. **Collaboration with Tech Industry**: Establish partnerships with technology companies and startups that are at the forefront of educational technology. These collaborations can provide early access to new technologies and insights into upcoming trends.

3. **Pilot Programs and Experimentation**: Implement pilot programs to test new technologies and gaming platforms in a controlled environment. This allows educators to assess the effectiveness and suitability of new tools before wider implementation.

4. **Feedback Loops**: Create systems for regular feedback from students, teachers, and parents on the use of technology in learning. This feedback is crucial for

understanding the impact of new technologies and for making informed decisions about future tech integration.

Addressing Digital Divide Issues
1. **Ensuring Equitable Access**: Work towards providing equitable access to digital resources and internet connectivity. This may involve seeking grants or funding to equip students with necessary devices or partnering with local businesses and community centers to provide access points.

2. **Inclusive Technology Planning**: Include considerations for the digital divide in technology planning and implementation strategies. This means considering the needs of all students, including those from lower-income families or remote areas.

3. **Alternative Learning Solutions**: Develop alternative solutions for students who may not have consistent access to digital tools at home. This could include providing printed materials, offering offline versions of digital games, or setting up after-school tech clubs.

Ethical and Privacy Considerations
1. **Data Privacy and Security**: Stay informed about data privacy laws and ethical standards, especially those concerning children's data, such as COPPA (Children's Online Privacy Protection Act). Ensure that all digital games and platforms used comply with these regulations.

2. **Transparency with Stakeholders**: Maintain transparency with parents and stakeholders about the types of data collected through educational games and how it is used. Obtain necessary consents and provide options for parents to opt-out if they have concerns.

3. **Ethical Use of AI and Adaptive Learning**: As AI and adaptive learning technologies become more prevalent, ensure their ethical use. This includes avoiding biases in AI algorithms and ensuring that adaptive learning systems are used to support, not replace, human teaching.

Fostering a Culture of Continuous Learning
1. **Encouraging Experimentation and Innovation**: Foster a culture where ed-

ucators are encouraged to experiment with new technologies and pedagogical approaches. Innovation should be seen as a valuable part of professional growth.

2. **Community and Network Building**: Build networks and communities of practice where educators can share experiences, challenges, and successes in integrating technology into teaching. This could be facilitated through online platforms or regular meetups.

3. **Policy Development and Advocacy**: Engage with policymakers to advocate for policies that support the integration of technology in education. This includes funding for tech resources, professional development programs, and research into effective educational technologies.

4. **Parental Engagement and Education**: Educate and involve parents in the technological transformation in education. This could include parent-focused workshops that showcase the benefits and potentials of digital game-based learning.

By preparing for future advancements and addressing challenges in digital game-based learning, educators and institutions can ensure that they not only keep pace with technological changes but also use these advancements to enhance and enrich early childhood education.

www.ingramcontent.com/pod-product-compliance
Lightning Source LLC
Chambersburg PA
CBHW031251290426
44109CB00012B/538